D1088302

BY THE SAME AUTHOR

Heraldry in the Catholic Church
Armorial Bruno Bernard Heim

OR AND ARGENT

by
Bruno Bernard Heim
of the
Académie Internationale d'Héraldique

Illustrated by the author

VAN DUREN
Gerrards Cross, 1994

First published in Great Britain in 1994
by Van Duren
an imprint of Colin Smythe Limited,
Gerrards Cross, Buckinghamshire,
England

British Library Cataloguing in Publication Data

A catalogue record for this book
is available from the British Library

ISBN 0-905715-24-1
ISBN 0-905715-36-5 limited signed edition

Produced in Great Britain

To
Alice and Cecil Humphery-Smith
with blessings and thanks
for their friendship
and
invaluable help

ACKNOWLEDGEMENTS

For their particularly useful help I owe thanks to:-
Bengt Olof Kälde, Uppsala,
Roy Lowlett, Canterbury,
Mikhail Yurievich Medvedev, St Petersburg,
Michael Schroeder, M.A., Frankfurt am Main,
and the late Cardinal Guido Del Mestri, who died in Nürnberg
on 2 August 1993.

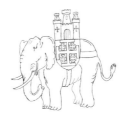

PREFACE

by His Grace The Duke of Norfolk, K.G.

To have a claim to the Kingdom of Jerusalem which hardly lasted a century, from 1099-1187, is awesome enough, but to find that, as Earl Marshal and head of the College of Heralds, in a special way one is contravening one of the text-book rules of heraldry is something very terrible.

As Lord Beaumont, a title first held in 1309 and which I inherited from my Mother, I am descended from Henry of Acre, younger son of Louis de Brienne whose father John was King of Jerusalem and Emperor of Constantinople (1210-1225). Henry was Vicomte of Beaumont in Maine, France, by right of his wife Agnes, daughter and eventual heiress of Raoul Vicomte of Beaumont.

The ancient arms of Beaumont were Azure, semy de lys and a lion rampant or (probably earlier versions had crosses rather than fleurs de lys). That coat was quartered with the arms attributed to Godfroy (Geoffrey) of Boulogne, King of the Crusaders' Kingdom of Jerusalem. Godfroy's coat of arms which appears in manuscripts of the thirteenth century was Silver or White with a Gold Cross between four or five other gold crosses. Placing gold charges on a silver field, so I am told, contravenes a basic rule of heraldry; but this was special in being the arms or insignia of the Church.

In *Or And Argent*, my good friend, Archbishop Bruno Heim, who was Papal Nuncio in England for many years and who has had a passion for heraldry since childhood, has, in his mid-eighties, produced a work of considerable scholarship and much humour denouncing the rule with more than adequate examples from all nations and heraldic styles to show that it was very often not respected except in the literature of coat armory.

Norfolk

INTRODUCTION

Most manuals written about heraldry place great emphasis on the 'sacred' rule that on a shield, colour must not appear upon colour, nor metal upon metal.

That the colour rule is very often ignored, particularly in Italian and French heraldry cannot go unnoticed by anyone who looks through armorials. In fact, there are many instances of arms with colour upon colour and colour alongside colour to be found also in British, German, Swiss and Eastern-European heraldry. The rule is more often asserted than observed, and this is accepted with fewer contradictions than when metals are in question.

It is not necessary, nor would it be possible to quote all the heraldic handbooks which deal with the rule (and often contain illustrations that discredit what they have affirmed). There are literally many tens of thousands of books and monographs which deal with heraldry, and no researcher could ever lay claim to having produced a complete bibliography. It is possible that some noteworthy author has given additional information about the rule, but unfortunately, I have not found it.

It is customary and easy for every petty writer to reiterate the rule while failing to give any account of its origin and significance and, above all, without taking the trouble to check the actual application of the rule throughout the centuries and consider its application in each country.

It is often asserted that the rule existed almost ready-made in early heraldic times. Pastoureau in his *Traité d'Héraldique* (1979 and 1993, p.109) says, however, that 'the origin of the rule remains mysterious, but it is certain that it has existed since armorial ensigns first appeared.' That would mean since the XIIth century.

My quest, therefore, is to discover if possible who invented the rule, who first mentioned it, how it was proved effective and sustained, and how, in fact, it was observed in each country where heraldry has been practised. So this present study is going to be a kind of detective story.

Can one understand why authorities insist so much more on keeping the metal rule than the equivalent colour rule? Azure or gules and vert or sable being side by side (or even one upon another) are less easily distinguishable than when gold and silver are put together. Nevertheless, sins against the colour rule are much more frequent than those against the metal rule and appear to be more easily forgiven.

To make the former 'mistake' more acceptable by calling it *cousu* is only a subterfuge and makes no difference. As distinguishability is given as and IS the reason for the famous rule, it makes little or no difference if metals or colours are **upon** or **next** to each other, i.e. touching each other.

To pretend that the arms of the King of Jerusalem are the only admitted and existing exception, as many authors do, seems to be arbitrary. One has to ask, were these colours of yellow and white to be seen on a shield or on a banner when Geoffrey bore them (c.1100)?

This 'exception' was created in pre- or proto-heraldic times, so it was an 'exception' to what in 1100? An exception to something that only later was going to exist. I have found no contemporary text saying that it was meant to be for all time the only legitimate 'exception'.

If we accept that the Boulogne/Jerusalem arms dated from the end of the XIth century this has been said *a posteriori*, decades later. If any colleague is aware of a nearly contemporary text or a means of finding one, I would be grateful to hear about it. I have searched very many books and manuscript documents, but the heraldic literature is so extensive that nobody can know it all. Even so, there must surely be, say, ten times as many instances of arms showing metal upon metal than I have seen myself. I do not hesitate to make this claim because every time I look I find more.

Next, we have to examine what heraldists of our own time and what those of past centuries have had to say about the colour and metal rules.

Having examined so many texts I shall only quote some of the most important and interesting authors. We shall see that in the past many have presented, and even copied from each other, a colour-philosophy which we, today, can only consider as far-fetched and often (not to be too unkind) rather infantile.

THE CONTEMPORARIES

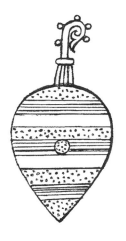

p.120, the arms of Dionysius de Bar, Bishop of Saint-Papoule, 1468 in the Cathedral of Bourges

The only well-known author who has presented a study in depth about the social history and cultural function of colours in an heraldic context is Michel Pastoureau in his *Figures et Couleurs, Images et Symboles*. In his *Traité d'Héraldique* he gives a statistical comparison of the heraldic usage and combination of colours (1993, pp.117-119). Nearly everywhere the coincidence of Or and Vert, and of Argent and Vert, are found to be the rarest, roughly one per cent of all arms.* But we have seen in quite a number of armorials that there are more frequent examples of the combination of Or and Argent, often twice as many as there are than Or or Argent joined with Vert.

Pastoureau in *Figures, et Couleurs, Images et Symboles* states (p.44) 'la règle d'empoi dès couleurs interdit de superposer' [and I am glad that he also says] 'ou *juxtaposer* [my italics] deux couleurs appartenant au même groupe'. 'Cette règle fortement contraignante existe dès l'apparition des armoiries au milieu du XIIe siècle, et a toujours et partout été respectée' (p.46).

My good friends, Galbreath and Jéquier, in *Lehrbuch der Heraldik* (1978, p.91) (and also in Galbreath's French books, for he was perfectly fluent in English, French and German), express themselves very objectively: 'the fundamental rule requires that one does not put colour on colour, nor metal on metal. We shall see, however, that there were always exceptions to this rule, and even very old ones, although it is based on the very reasonable understanding of visibility'.

* This is not found to be the case in Holland: in Rietstap's *Wappenboek van den Nederlandoschen Adel* we find among 616 arms illustrated:
26 Or and Argent (over 4%)
30 Or and Vert (5%)
31 Argent and Vert (over 5%)
Neither in Portugal: we find in Du Cros's *Livro do Armeiro-Mor* among 300 arms:
8 Or and Argent
18 Or and Vert
24 Argent and Vert
And in Santos Fereira's *Armorial Português* among 1500:
9 Or and Argent (0.6%)
63 Or and Vert (4%)
84 Argent and Vert (5.6%)
Also in Italy and Ireland the Or-Vert and Argent-Vert combinations are very frequent.

Siddons, in *The Development of Welsh Heraldry* (1991) p.232, writes 'That the Welsh did not concern themselves with the niceties of the rule against putting colour on colour . . . can easily be seen by consulting Syr Tomas ab Ieuan ap Deicws's little armorial in blazon, or Gruffudd Hiraethog's recordings of arms in houses and churches'. Quoting Peniarth MS 127 & 136 he mentions instances of colour on colour, and metal on metal arms between 1485 and 1246, the latter from Llanstephan MS 46. On p.233, however, Siddons quotes Humphrey Llwyd of Denbigh (+1568) 'who expressly states in his *Dosbarth Arfau* "metal should not be put on metal, nor colour on colour" . . . But the instructions given to Gruffudd Hiraethog by the Kings of Arms for his visitations do not mention specifically the rules against metal on metal and colour on colour'.

Fox-Davies, in his *Complete Guide to Heraldry*, (1909) p.85, says, 'colour cannot be placed upon colour nor metal upon metal. This is a definite rule which must practically always be rigidly observed. Many writers go so far as to say that the only case of an infraction of this rule will be found in the arms of Jerusalem'. He quotes Woodward who enumerates twenty instances of the violation of the rules. 'The whole of these instances, however, are taken from continental armory, in which this exception – for even on the Continent such *Armes Fausses* are noticeable exceptions - occur more frequently than in this country'.

'Nevertheless, such exceptions do occur in British armory, and the following instances of well-known coats which break the rule may be quoted' - and he cites several.

Fox-Davies then blazons two colour on colour arms of Lloyd of Ffoss-y-Bleidied (1164) and of Meredith Takery (p.86), and he continues saying 'a little careful research, no doubt, would produce a large number of English instances, but one is bound to admit the possibility that the great bulk of these cases may really be instances of augmentations'.

Such instances, of course, are not considered in this book. There are enough genuine English ones, and indeed more research would produce many which are generally overlooked. Even in France, where the rule probably comes from and where it is most frequently repeated, yet is shown as much disrespect as everywhere else, many 'exceptions' are to be found.

EARLIER AUTHORS

WOODWARD (1892) is rather prudent, but he also thinks that the 'wrongdoers' are mainly continental. He says (p.102): 'It is a primary fundamental canon of Heraldry that metal is not to be placed upon metal, nor colour on colour. This is the one heraldic rule with which all persons seem to be acquainted, and which has become almost a proverbial saying: "Metal on metal is false heraldry", etc. This rule, no doubt, originated in the necessity for securing distinctiveness in the days when arms were actually borne on the military shield, surcoat and banners and when it was of the utmost importance that they should be easily distinguishable from afar off.'

Evidently, from an artistic as well as from a practical point of view, if Or and Argent were to come together in a shield, one should not use a feeble lemon yellow but a strong, saturated chrome. But then many, especially British, heraldists tend to call it 'proper', just to avoid in words the falseness of which the arms would be accused.

'But the interdiction is far from absolute. The arms of the Kingdom of Jerusalem . . . are the best known instance (sometime even it is asserted to be the *only* instance) of a permitted violation of the rule . . . In this and a few other cases, the arms are styled *arma inquirenda* or *armes pour enquérir*, and it is asserted that they were originally composed for the express purpose of causing the beholder to enquire the reason of such an infraction of heraldic usage, and so to stamp them in his memory. When a limited view is taken . . . such assertions seem capable of easy justification. In our own country, for instance, distinct violations . . . are of great rarity' (p. 103).

This is an easy self-deception. There are illustrations here of a few British instances, and we have seen hundreds more. More and more are found while examining further armorials and manuscripts and visiting churches. Yet we cannot go on *ad infinitum*, we would never come to an end.

'But when the student extends his view over the much larger field of continental heraldry he finds such assertions quite unwarrantable ... The exceptions which the present writer [Woodward] has collected may be counted by the hundred rather than by the dozen ... and the idea that they were intended as *armes pour enquérir* cannot be entertained' (p.103).

On his plates, Woodward shows a number of 'exceptions': Plate V 6, Lowell; Plate VII 7, Haldermansteten; Plate IX 1, Jerusalem; Plate X 6, Orsini; Plate XII 5, Sanchez; Plate XV 6, Montfort; Plate XVIII 5, Mortimer; Plate XXI 1, Venice; Plate XXXI 5, Bertie; Plate LV 3, Eyfelsberg.

BOUTELL writes in his *Manual of Heraldry* (p. 43) 'It is a strict law, that a charge of metal must rest upon a field that is of a colour; or contrariwise . . . that is, *that metal be not on metal, nor colour on colour.* This rule is modified in the case of *varied fields,* upon which may be charged a bearing of either a metal or a colour: also a partial relaxation of the rule is conceded when one bearing is charged upon another, should the conditions of any particular case require such a concession.'

'This rule is not so rigidly enforced in Foreign Heraldry; but in the Heraldry of England, the solitary intentional violation of it is the *silver* armorial shield of the crusader Kings of Jerusalem.'

That is not a particularly English example but it is mentioned and repeated by many English and foreign authors!

Count Amédée DE FORAS (1883) says on p.113 of his book *Le Blason:* one of the best-known rules is that one ought never to put colour on colour, nor metal on metal.

He thinks one should cry 'murder' if one finds this rule deliberately misused. He admits, however, that there exist many exceptions to the rule and he is inclined to regard them as 'acceptable exceptions'.

We agree with him, as long as there is provision to allow for minor details such as a small coronet on the head of an animal, and for tongues and claws. We also think that chequy, lozengy and compony pieces do not disturb visibility, and are therefore generally admitted as colour on colour and metal on metal. Also, the rule does not apply to quarterings of different arms brought together in one shield. However, we would say that the rule is violated and does apply when a coat of arms is simply quartered: for instance, Azure and Gules, but we would never agree when there is a question of overall (*sur le tout*). In these cases colour passes over colour or metal over metal, which is clearly UPON, contrary to the rule.

De Foras (1883) gives absolution also to 'coupés' (per fess) and 'partis' (per pale) colour on colour. This is by many considered an offence, and it is indeed contrary to the rule. The word 'cousu' does not make it any better, but it is very frequent in French blazoning.

DUBUISSON, for example, in his *Armorial Alphabétique* (1757) has well over 150 instances of arms showing colour abutting colour: 'cousus' and more unpardonables, such as Sable on Vert, and Sable on Azure. Further, he has a score of examples of Or on Argent.

We have to repeat that the breach of the colour rule is much more frequent than the breach of the metal rule inspite of their being against the same one and equivalent rule. For French breaches, see also Vicomte de Magny (Plate XV) and *Annuaire Universel*, (Plate XVII).

There is surely no need to insist any more that these authors state the rule and then ignore the evidence which we can now examine.

SPENER, in *Insignium Theoria* (1690), *Pars* 1, *Cap* IV, p.118, XXVII states: 'Regulas quod concernit, Bartolus ... & alii jubent semper metallum & colores digniores potiori, hoc est superiori vel dextro loco locari. Sed regulam hanc numquam receptam esse mille contraria exempla evincunt'.

§ XXVIII. 'In istam vero legem conspirasse plerosque populos ... reperimus, qua metallum, metallo, colorem colori inscribi prohibetur ... Quod causam huius legis attinet risum an indignationem meliori jure mereatur ineptia Feroni, ... lector judicet: cum iste fabulatur, Adamo solum colorem rubrum quia ex terra rubra ejus ortus, & eadem significatio nominis pro insigni datum, dein lapsu secuto pomum nigrum demonstrandae turpitudini peccati injectum esse: ob quod majores insignia in quibus color colori incumbat, falsitatis damnarint. Uti vero palam et, hanc rationem ineptissimam esse ... neutiquam laboro'.

Spener writes extensively about metals and colours. His text is in Latin, mixed with some French and German. He is quoting Bartolus, Upton, Vulson de la Colombière, de Bado Aureo and, of course, Ménestrier.

Evidently, Spener is not a great friend of rules because he knows too many exceptions, of which he blazons a number in his footnotes. Those who insist dogmatically on the rules pardon so many more breaches apart from those which every one accepts.

It is not easy to distil the juice of Spener's rather confusing and complicated treatise, but in order not to make it too long, we translate some of his most expressive explanations:

§ XXVII. Having given an order of seniority to metals and colours, e.g. gold before silver, blue before black, he continues 'Concerning the rules, Bartolus and others order that the more worthy metals and colours should be given the better place, i.e.

in chief or on the dexter. But a thousand contrary examples eliminate this rule'!!

§ XXVIII. Discussing the metal and colour rule in question, he states, 'Yet in this law we find most people conspiring . . . that it is prohibited to paint metal on metal and colour on colour . . . As to the reason for this law the reader might judge if the ineptitude of Feronus deserves laughter rather than indignation when he tells the yarn that Adam is given only the red colour as his insignia, because he is made of red soil, and after his downfall a black apple to demonstrate the turpitude of the sin: wherefore, "majores insignia, in quibus color colori incumbat, falsitatis damnarint".

'[Does he mean] "wherefore, most have condemned as false insignia [those arms] in which colour lies upon colour" [?] As it is evident that this argument is ridiculous, I have no intention of taking any more trouble indicating and condemning other [arguments]. I rather concur with Ponto who says the custom is confirmed by long usage and therefore the observation of the law is inevitable'.

'One should pay special attention to the colours, and that every colour should be incorporated in arms according to its significance, and that yellow and white are used as the most noble ones, because among many thousands of arms none can be found which would not be adorned and set up with yellow or white. Nevertheless, few are found with both the mentioned colours such as those of the Reichsedlen [nobles of the Empire] Landschaden von Steinach. For: Or signifies wisdom, desire, joy and fidelity; Argent instead: innocence, purity, honesty and eloquence. The reason is based on the hypothesis that the [coats of] arms originated from the clothes of the old soldiery. Hereonwards derives the reason for the heraldic axiom that metal should not be painted on metal, nor colour on colour. For who would weave a silver thread in a golden tissue without doing great damage to value and beauty? Therefore, also weaving and embroidering have their place in this branch and many heraldic dogmas are taught and proved by such reasoning'.

We do not know who Feronus and Ponto were. Spener goes on at great length. His writing is accordingly abbreviated here to make it understandable because his Latin, German and French are obsolete. Translation into modern English cannot be literal.

16

Now let us ask: are these convincing reasons why in heraldry metal should not be put on metal? Spener provides the answer by saying that 'founded on similar considerations heraldic dogmas are taught or proved'.

For most people the only plausible reason for the metal-colour rule is that it makes for better visibility, but heraldists through the centuries have concocted some of the most ridiculous imaginable reasons for the rule. Readers should be amused by some examples.

On p.119 Spener quotes le Laboureur's *De L'Origine Des Armes* saying (n.101) 'une certaine obscurité morne & sombre, qui resulte de l'affinité de couleurs & métaux mal assortis, qui les prive de l'esclat & de la splendeur, qu'ils recevroient par le voisinage de quelqu'autre émail plus opposé'. So that the falsity would only be seen in the unpleasant combination of colours and metals.

'But this is rejected by Ménestrier, *L'art de Blason Justifié* C.13 p. 343. calling [such arms] false and adulterous'.

To this Spener says with too many entangled words: 'but really (*verum enim vero*) one would not be wrong in doubting if it is justified to put to shame and accuse of falsity those who made themselves arms deviating from this canon (*canonem hunc impegere*)'.

Then he quotes nine legitimate exceptions, of which some, to my mind, frustrate the rule.

He also mentions the problem of furs, in particular of Ermine, which, as far as visibility is concerned, is nearer to white (Argent) than to any colour. But in blazoning to avoid mentioning gold next to silver, one says Ermine and Argent and Ermine and Or; yet what difference does this wording make to what one can see when white is next to white and white next to gold?

On page 120 § XXX, Spener mentions as an exception to the rule blazoning charges as 'proper' (*au naturel*) a term which is said to have been assumed 'pour éviter la fausseté' – in order to avoid falsity. Using such tricks of language makes no real difference except a verbal one. 'Proper' is very seldom used in German blazonry. It is, however, frequent in French and British blazoning. I have seen in a colour illustrated book a white swan when on colour blazoned Argent and in the same book, when on yellow (Or) blazoned Proper.

Spener finds this expedient ludicrous and to make it evident he mentions Vulson calling a red crayfish on a blue shield 'Azure a boiled crayfish'! This, of course, is in order to avoid having to admit that it is a case of colour upon colour, Gules upon Azure. Does this insincerity save the rule?

On page 121 § XXXI, we read 'and yet we have not finished because they note that the divisions of a shield can be of two metals so that only the charges set on the shield, but not the divisions of a shield, are considered by the rule'. This is correct if the divisions (impalememts or quarterings) bear the charges of two or more different arms, but it is not so when the divisions constitute one achievement as, for example, Quarterly, Or and Argent, a lion rampant Gules overall; or, Per pale Or and Argent, a charge of a colour overall.

Page 122 § XXXII: 'Another exception close to the former is the 9th – "quod nonnumquam ipsae figurae, quas honorabiles vocant, alit[er] quam regula poscere videbatur, solo inscribuntur".' This is poor Latin and not easily understandable. It becomes clearer when we read one of the instances he quotes: 'caput adsutum rubeum imponitur scuto caeruleo': Azure a chief *cousu* Gules. To that he observes 'The French (*pour cacher la fausseté*) call this *cousu*'.

This is very frequent in French armory and the fact that they call it 'cousu' shows that they are conscious of the irregularity. This is precisely what we wish to expose, namely the oft-repeated rule which is so fanatically defended with fallacious arguments by its supporters and by those who blindly pretend it to be absolute law. Colour upon colour is as much against the rule as metal upon metal and makes visible distinction even more difficult.

JOHN GIBBON, in his *Introductio ad Latinam Blasoniam* (1682) is far from being a defender of the metal and colour rule. He quotes (p.6) the following poem:

> 'But Nileus, he who with a forged stile
> Vaunted to be the Son of sevenfold Nile,
> And bare seven Silver Rivers in his Shield
> Distinctly waving through a Golden Field'

'Neither is this my Quotation impertinent to make out that the Heralds are too hard and severe in obstinately maintaining that a Field or Shield of Arms must not be all colour or all Metal, unless in some extraordinary cases'.

'Bartolus says, *Sicut nomina inventa sunt ad cognoscendum homines, ita et Insignia ad idem inventa sunt.'*

'Now if Arms, as well as Names, were devised for distinction sake . . . and Colours are as much distinctive as Metals, such a Coat of Arms is no such peccant thing, as we are made to believe'.

On p.150, Gibbon writes 'I have defended Arms Colour on Colour, Metal on Metal: Now for my Readers diversion and delight, I will insert what has fallen under my observation'. He quotes from Ferne, 'Worthy of all Credit and Belief', thirty instances 'seen in Churches and Chapels' of which we give here only three Or and Argent examples:

On p.150 'Argent three Lys Or, in Bedenham Church near Bedford'. On the same page he says, 'My self observed (in Flaughton Church in Suffolk) Bl. on a Bend Argent three Pheons Or', and two pages later, 'Argent three Rests Or.'

After he quotes Prov. 25, 11:

'Argentea poma Solo aureo depicta: which brings to my mind a notable Passage in *Stow, Anno* 1345 (taken out of Sir *Thomas de la More) viz*: That the Lord Prior of the *Carmelite* Fryers of our Lady of Tholouse, displayed a Banner of our Lady in Gold set in a Field of Silver, provoking the French men to Arms: . . . I could instance many Outlandish Coats of this nature, but these may suffice; only let me add, That if *Labels,*

Chiefs, Cantons, Bordures may be Colour on Colour, Metal on Metal, why not other Essentials?' This I find logical thinking without any unnecessary stubborn prejudice.

Gibbon makes some further observations with which I am not the only one who would gladly agree: on page 96 (*Camdeni Blasoniæ*) he quotes the following blazoning:

'*Lucii: tres lucios pisces in rubro clypeo gestabant* – Gules three Luces proper – Here is omitted the colour of the Fishes, as being to be understood *nativi coloris*, which is Argent or very near thereto'.

Also, what he writes about Ermine (on p.112, *Vredi Blasoniæ*) is most sensible. Blazoning BRETAGNE 'Scutum Pontici muris vellere descriptum: Ermine, or as the French have it, Argent semé of Ermines Sable'.

'The Ermines Skin is not spotted all over, but only at the very tip of its Tail; therefore this Coat were more properly blazoned *Scutum argenteum, maculis Pontici muris interstinctum*'.

SILVANUS MORGAN, Arms-Painter says in his *Armilogia sive Ars Chromatica* (1666) (p.2): 'Colour upon colour is false Heraldry, and it was palpable even at the first creation, when darkness was upon the face of the deep: for that was Colour without Metal.'

'When Jove hides Heaven in clouds, and sullen Night makes no distinction 'twixt the Black and White.'

'Metal upon Metal is false Heraldry, because they invade each others dignity, both OR AND ARGENT, being of celestial extraction, and in their own Houses have more essential dignities than in each others; for then there is a Metal without a colour.'

Not only Jove is a guarantor of the rule, God has 'filled the Shield of the Universe with either Animal, Vegetative, or Mineral Bodies . . .'.

'The Field is, that is to say, the Colour of the Shield . . .' (p.3) while 'some ascribe the true nature to the graduality of opacity and light'.

'... If you consider the colours Elementarily, then the Black or SABLE is to be preferred *propter antiquitatem & fundamentum*; but if in the second notion in the graduity of opacity and light. Then the Red Colour or *gules* being made by a greater proportion of light mingled with darkness, must be preferred before the *azure* or Blue, being mingled with a less proportion of light mingled with darkness'.

'The reason why no Coat of Arms can be said good without Metal is because Light of all things in the World is the most powerful Agent upon our Eye ... for where Light is not, Darkness is'.

'Colour is nothing else but Light mingled with Darkness' (p.4).

Light 'in this Art is called Argent. It expresses IMMACULATUM unspotted ... it is the Messenger of Peace, and deserves the first place ... it simply signifies the everlasting charity of the Almighty, and in moral virtues Piety, Virginity, clear Conscience and Charity' (p.6).

Or, Gold 'is a fit bearing for dignified persons; in God it signifieth *illum regnare majestate indutum et celsitudine*; He being clothed with Majesty and Might, of itself it betokens Wisdom, Justice, Riches, and Elevation of Mind' (p.7).

'Metal and colour make a perfect Coat of Armour.'

With this all heraldists agree, but all Morgan's explanations involving God Almighty, Jove, Neptune, Apollo, David, Aristotle, Virgil, Horace, Ovid, Plato and the Apostles provide me with no reason as to why Or and Argent could not stand together.

On the contrary it reminds me of Spener's dictum, mentioned above: 'the reader may decide whether this foundation of the law deserves laughter rather than indignation'.

Has now the detective story reached the final solution? Further back than Morgan has ventured – to the Creation – no one can go!

FRANÇOIS CLAUDE MÉNESTRIER, a French Jesuit (often quoted by Spener, who had visited him in France) who between

1659 and 1696 published nine heraldic books, is a more severe defender of the rule than Spener. He is sure about it without giving long and silly reasons for it as many other authors do. His doctrine is:

'One always puts metal on colour or colour on metal, that is, Or or Argent on azure, gules, vert, sable: or the contrary azure, gules, vert, sable on Or or Argent. When the shield is of colour the figures must be of metal and when the field is metal the figures must be colour.'

'There are, however, so-called false arms about which one must enquire because there is colour on colour, metal on metal. They are called false because they are against the common usage. One must enquire if there was a special privilege or another reason like for the arms of Jerusalem'.

The custom of putting colour on metal and metal on colour, according to Ménestrier, comes from the ancient clothing made of multicoloured tissues. One imagined in olden times that not all colours matched well together 'except white and yellow which come nearest to gold and silver and this could be mixed or mistaken with the other colours'. Does this make sense?

The quotation is translated from pages 14 and 215 of the German edition of *La Science de la noblesse ou la nouvelle méthode du blason* published in Ulm, 1694. It must be intended to say that metal on metal (yellow and white) are not very distinct and that this would impair visibility, which is the only valid reason for the rule.

In fact, the earliest known woven fabrics of heraldic-like designs are of damask cloth in which visibility is subtle and even white on white and gold upon gold show the patterns clearly. Perhaps the Jerusalem 'exception' was nothing else in origin but a repetition for the Cross in gold upon silver damascene engraving or on white damask twill.

It is interesting to note that Ménestrier says that metal on metal arms could be given 'by privilege' which would imply that it derived from some special favour.

PETRA SANCTA

p. 72
Darpo
Venetia

p. 86
in Aragon. Regio
stemmate et
cancellarius
Nemoursiorum
instemmate
Ducum Sabaudiae

The Roman Jesuit Silvester Petra Sancta is a well known heraldic scholar. He (not Vulson de La Colombière) invented the system indicating the heraldic tinctures by different hatchings (see Douët D'Arcq, p. 263, and also Palliot, p. 34).

John Christoph Gatterer in *Handbuch der Heraldik* (1763) p. 215, says that Jacob Francquart used a kind of hatching as early as 1623, but it is Petra Sancta's system which has been consistently practised ever since.

In his *Tesserae Gentilitiae* (1638) he mentions the rule, but says, however, that there are noble arms with two metals or two colours, 'infrequentes tamen sunt, sed inveniuntur eae tamen', they are not frequent but they also do exist.

In his illustrations he shows us more than sixty Or-Argent instances from all over Europe.

Here follow some examples . . .

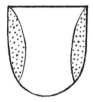

p. 87
Gulielm.
Angl.
(quoting
Leigh)

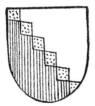

p. 211
Bonizzi
Florentiae

p. 255
Allegrini Atrebatis
Galliae cancellarius
Silesia

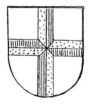

p. 308
Hesseniorum,
Silesia

JOHN GUILLIM (1565-1621) is said to be 'the first who brought method into this Heroic Art'. His *A Display of Heraldry* (1611) was published in many editions after his death, augmented by various authors who traded on his name, in 1632, 1638, 1660, 1679 and 1724.

In Section I, Chapter III, he speaks about general rules of Blazon and Colours.

'All colours are different mixtures of white and black', as Johannes de Bado Aureo already said more than two hundred years before Guillim. One wonders if both were colour blind! As a painter of arms I cannot agree with that. Mixtures of black and white never become yellow, red, blue or green, but only different shades of grey. However, all colours of the spectrum are of different degrees of brightness between white and black; or so it could be said.

Guillim begins by treating white (silver, Argent) and yellow (gold, Or), followed by the other heraldic colours, but he does not mention the rule.

In the fifth edition (1679) published long after Guillim's death, his text is repeated word for word, but on p.11 (corresponding to p. 9 in his original text) Richard Blome, who has been described as 'a literary adventurer', interpolated fourteen lines saying that 'Armory cannot be good, that hath not in it either *Gold* or *Silver*'. On p. 227 of this fifth edition we find this illustration blazoned: 'Or a Pillar Sable enwrapped by an Adder Argent, by the Name of Myntur'.

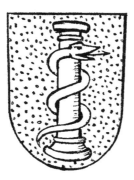

In the sixth edition, 'improved with large additions', of 1724 more than a hundred years after Guillim's death, in Chapter III, p.12, the rule is largely explained. This, although published under his name, cannot be attributed to the 'worthy and well-deserving Master J. Guillim'.

In this Chapter we also read: 'It is an indisputable Rule in Heraldry, as Mackenzie p.20 observes, That Colour and Metal must be us'd or else Furr to supply the want of one, and that Colour cannot be put immediately upon Colour, nor Metal upon Metal.'

'This Rule was not taken notice of by the Romans . . . But this Law was first authorised by Charles the Great, and afterwards improv'd . . . it is now stated by Heralds: in legibus Heraldicis non convenit Metallum supra Metallum ponere, ita quoque non decet colores supra colores pingere'.

'The reason why this Use became a Law was from the several Colours us'd by Soldiers, and others in their Habits . . . For it being a Custom to embroider Gold or Silver upon Silk, or Silk upon cloth of Gold or Silver, therefore it was afterwards appointed, That in imitation of the Cloaths so embroider'd, Colours should not be us'd upon Colour, nor Metal upon Metal; and not from the Differences which fell out in the Trojan War, betwixt the Followers of Achilles and Ulysses, whereupon Achilles's friends blason'd only Metals, and Ulysses's Friends colours'.

I cannot see any logical connection. Ménestrier made the statement decades before this sixth edition of Guillim and he has often simply been repeated. To enforce the rule many different and irrelevant reasons have been produced which often make no sense to the enquiring mind of any present-day scholar. The rule is generally accepted for reasons of common sense but those given for it in the later editions of Guillim are very unconvincing.

What has Greek mythology to do with heraldry? Why should Charlemagne issue heraldic laws 400 years before heraldry began? Why should the embroidering of gold and silver, which was done in ancient times, become a reason for not doing it in armory later on?

In E.B(LUNT)'s *The Elements of Armories* (1610), there is talk of the dignity and meaning of the Colours (in which the metals are expressly included).

On p.168 he says merrily, 'one of the colours must be a metal. Against that there are nevertheless examples even from old time'.

In BARTELEMY VINCENT's *Le Blason des Armoiries* (1581) he writes, of course, extensively about metals and colours: 'Or is the most noble of all the metals. It signifies faith, strength, confidence, nobility, richness, goodwill, comfort, highness, solidity, purity, splendour and satisfaction'.

'Argent in blazon stands for hope, purity, humility, beauty, victory, felicity and blankness'.

Vincent does not mention the rule, however. Among his rather good illustrations we find Or, two anchors in saltire Argent, their nowed cables Gules, (p.64); Quarterly Or and Argent, a cross moline Gules in the centre of the chief (p.70); Argent, a chief Azure, over all a lion Or (p.120); Or, a raven Argent (p.125); The Jerusalem Cross without any comment (p.126).

LE JARDIN D'ARMOIRIES (1567) edited by Gheraert Salenson in Ghent, is thought to be the first armorial to have been put into print which included both illustration and blazoning.

| p. E.V | p. F.III | p. E.III | p. F.V | p. H.III |

In this small volume we have on p.E.V
BARRAT: d'argent a trois malletes d'or.

p. F. III BRANDENBURG: d'argent a aigle d'or.

p. E. III BAES: d'argent a trois étoils d'or, & un poisson d'argent.

p. F. V BRIDEGENT: d'or à griffon d'argent.

p. H. III CASSENBORGH: d'argent a trois faucilles d'or manchées de gueulles.

GERARD LEIGH, in his *The Accedens of Armorie* (1562 and 1612), talks scrupulously about the heraldic tinctures and their symbolic meaning, yet he says nothing about the rule or about incompatibility. His work is composed in the classical tutorial form of a dialogue betwee the supposed Master, Gerard, and his Pupil, Leigh.

On p.5 we read

'[Gerard] Now I will onely show the composition, or joyning of metall or colour with Gold as followeth:

SIMPLE
1. But simple, first it signifieth as before is rehearsed (Or signifieth wisdom, riches, magnanimity, joyfulness, elevation of mind).

2. WITH ARGENT, to be a victor over all infidels, Turkes, and Sarazins.

3. With Gules ... 4. With Azure ... 5. With Sable ... 6. With Verte ... 7. With Purpure ...

[Leigh] I perceive you well. Go now to the second Metall (p.6)

[Gerard] That is called silver and blazed by the name of Argent ... (p.7) Simply of itself it signifieth to the bearer thereof; chastity, virginity, clear conscience and charity.

Compounded,

2. With Or, to revenge Christ's bloodshed.

3. With Gules, bold in all honesty.

4. With Azure ... 5. With Sable ... 6. With Verte ... 7. With Purpure ...

[Leigh] I pray you satisfie me in one thing that I will aske you, whereby I may rather understand your compounds. For in your compounds of Gold with all other, you have set the Sylver, and shewing your meaning thereof, in that place your saying is, with Sylver, and here ye say with Gold, and to mine understanding, they ought both have one meaning.

(p . 8)

[Gerard] It might seem so to the unskilfull, but you must understand, that in the treaty of Gold, where I say with Argent, which is as much to say, as with Silver, the Gold is there first. So here in this place, when I say with Or (which is to be understood with Gold) the Silver is first. For that must be a generall rule unto you for the first naming of everie thing. For therein standeth a preheminence.

[Leigh] I do now understand you. As though the field of the Scocheon, were of both these metals, of which ... there should be a regard, and that is shewed by the meaning of this word (whith). Well now I pray you to proceede, and shew me of the seven colours'.

On p. 59 Leigh shows the Arms of Jerusalem and blazons:

'He beareth Argent a Crosse croslet Or.
This is otherwise added a Jerusalem crosse,
as be borne of Godfrey de Bulleine.'

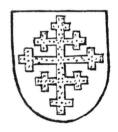

Leigh writes nothing more, nothing about a reason, nothing about it being an exception.

In his *Heraldry in School Manuals of the Middle Ages*, Cecil R. Humphery-Smith, writes: 'The study of heraldry was a normal part of the curriculum of law students in the Middle Ages'. The 'Sloane Tract' (British Library Manuscript *Sloane* 3744) is written in archaic English and Latin. 'The handwriting is not earlier than the second half of the fifteenth century, probably 1470 or somewhat later.' It is thought not to be a copy

28

of the Ashmolean Tract (Bodleian Library Manuscript Ashmole 75A). 'More likely ... each was a "text-book" or "lecture-notes-book" on heraldry written by students of the same ... heraldry master".'

Then we read, 'there are no arms unless there is silver and gold in them' and 'one must not place metal upon metal *nor metal upon ermine* [my italics]: likewise not colour upon colour'.

I always felt that Ermine gives the impression of white and should be treated as white (Argent), but this is not the meaning of the rule-enthusiasts because Ermine and Or verbally does not say Argent (white) and Or (yellow) and so the furs are safe from the rule. It is, however, hardly easier to distinguish it from some distance. And as visibility is the only valid reason for the rule Ermine should not be treated as a colour. It should more obviously be seen as it looks and not be included in the much defended rule.

Is it the appearance or the wording that should be decisive? Is the sound more important in heraldry than visibility? Is not there sometimes a glimmer of hypocrisy in the maintenance of the rule at any cost such as in the frequent use of 'proper'? A shield is for the eye to see, not for the ear to hear! Nevertheless, a lyrical blazon does no harm if it accurately describes what one sees.

This is, in fact, the first time I find the rule applied to Ermine. Nearly 200 years later Spener mentions the problem, but the enthusiasts for the rule find even Ermine on Argent correct. The rule is verbally saved but not for the eye; and in heraldry the appearance is more important than the verbal blazon!

NICOLAS UPTON was a Canon of Sarum (old Salisbury), and Wells Cathedral who compiled his treatise *De Studio Militari* in 1441. It was first published in 1486 and again in 1645 by Sir Edward Bysshe (Bissaeus). Bysshe was wrong in believing that Upton was the most ancient author in England to have written on the subject of heraldry, and was in error when he suggested that Upton could have been the author of the *Tractatus de armis* adopting the name of Johannes de Bado Aureo, who wrote his treatise before Upton was born, about the year 1400.

Upton had developed and amplified de Bado's tract, especially writing with almost tedious prolixity, 'de coloribus in armis depictis': WHAT IS COLOUR? THE ORIGINS OF

COLOURS: For an heraldist of our time it is a curiosity rather than of really pertinent interest that he sees the origins of colours founded on different proportions of humidity, of dryness, warmth and cold.

It is rather useless to follow his lengthy trend of thought. Let us simply quote some peculiarities: 'Snow is cold and white'. 'If the humidity is less and the heat great, great blackness can be produced (nigredo magna potest generari).' 'Sometimes however heat produces whiteness in humidity (quandoque tamen calidum generat albedinem in humido: ut patet in albedine ovi cocti) as one can see in the whiteness of a boiled egg'!

Why should we quote such deviations? After having spoken about the generation of colours, Upton dedicates five pages to white (Argent) and yellow (Or), before treating the other colours and in his long explanations about Argent and Or, he does not say a word about a rule or about the incompatibility of the two colours. He does not even call them metals.

BERNARD DU ROSIER: MS. 6020 in The Bibliothèque Nationale of Paris is a *Liber Armorum*. Its author presents himself as Bernardus de Rosergio, master of theology, doctor of law, provost of the metropolitan cathedral of Toulouse. He was for more than twenty years Professor of Law at Toulouse University. In 1451 he became Archbishop of Toulouse, it is likely that he wrote his *Liber Armorum* some time before that date. He died in 1474. The manuscript comprises thirty-one double pages of thirty lines each, folios 13-44. He begins his text with a list of contents. It is written in good medieval Latin. The first of the fifteen headings may be translated:

1. What are arms?

2. Why are they called arms?

3. What do arms signify?

4. Who has the right to bear arms?

5. Who can grant new arms?

6. To whom can new arms be granted and why?

7. How and in which forms arms must be composed.

8. With which colours arms must be painted and the colours in them, how must they be inserted and parted. (Quibus coloribus debent arma depingi et colores in eisdem quomodo debent inseri et partiri).

9. Which metals can be put in arms and in which order they must be placed. (Que metalla in armis possunt collocari et qualiter debent ordinari).

So, we have arrived at the section of special interest to us. The subject is treated on pages 22 and 23 of du Rosier's MS. The translated Latin text reads:

'Among all the metals only two are to be used in arms, viz: Or and Argent because they are the brightest and the noblest of metals. Or precedes Argent (in situatione et formatione armorum) in precedence and construction of arms, (et in eisdem armis sine alia mixtura colorum non se bene compaciuntur) and in the same arms without mixing with colour they are not compatible because one metal is confused by the other and its appearance obscured.

This is, indeed, the only good reason why arms of Or and Argent in juxtaposition are less frequently found than instances of metal with colour.

'That is why it is reputed that in any shield one of these two metals is enough. That is to say, Or or Argent, which is disregarded in the shield of arms of a King (fallit in scuto seu in armis regis . . .) in which are crosses Or and Argent together since the time of Geoffrey de Bouillon . . . in memory of the most gallant Conquest of the Holy Land by the aforesaid 'godofredum de billion' two metals were put in the arms of the kingdom of Jerusalem, and if any other would put these two metals in his arms, this would in fact be considered as false. Thus arms with other colours more apparent proportionately situated with these metals . . . are considered more noble and more dignified. Arms composed with metals and bright colours are nearer to light and clarity, which is evidently true.

Bernard du Rosier often quotes Bartolus but, of course, not in this section of his treatise.

A few lines further on he writes about clothing just as later authors do. He says that golden vestments are appropriate only for divine service, and for emperors, kings and princes of this world, but he does not state this in relation to the heraldic colour/metal rule as many later authors imagine.

On page 38, XXXVIII Rosier comes back to the topic, saying 'in the same arms or shields Or and Argent must not be put together; it is inconvenient and such arms are considered fictitious and not true, 'fictitia et non vera'. And then he mentions again the arms of 'Godofredus de billon [sic] post sanctam victoriosam conquistam civitatis Jerusalem et terre sancte'.

THE ARGENTAYE TRACT. Douët d'Arcq in his *Traité du Blason du XVe Siècle* presents the work of an anonymous author of the beginning of the XVth century whom he dates after 1418. The rule of never putting metal on metal nor colour on colour appears in the seventh chapter of this manuscript; pages 326 and 327, 'one must know that arms with metal on metal or colour on colour are false . . . Thereby, arms of people of low rank and non-nobles who without discretion take arms arbitrarilly are often recognised . . .'.

'In general all arms which are composed of metal on metal or colour on colour are false, except those of Jerusalem, in which metal is upon metal, that is, Argent a cross potent and four crosslets Or, yet nevertheless these are not false arms. And the reason is that when Geoffrey de Bouillon most victoriously had conquered the Holy Land he was advised by the valiant and brave princes who were in his company that in memory and remembrance of this excellent victory he should bear arms different from the common others so that when anyone might see them believing that they were false they might be moved to enquire why a so noble king bears such arms, and so can be informed of the aforesaid conquest'.

This was the common and oft repeated explanation. If somebody better read than myself has ever seen a contemporary (1100) account of this story, I would be grateful to be told of it. Until then, I am inclined to believe that when, for practical reasons, the heralds started proclaiming the rule, this explanation was invented. Surely, Geoffroy and his companions did not and could not mean to sanction a rule which became a guideline later. How could they foresee the development of heraldry? 'He was given arms different from the common': Was there a common heraldic practice in 1100? I think not!

SICILLE, herald of Alphonso V, King of Aragon, in his treatise *Le Bason des Couleurs*, written in Mons between 1435 and 1458, answers questions asked by an imaginary pursuivant.

'I tell you', he says, 'Every shield (armoirie) is made of one of the five colours mentioned before and of one metal on the shield or *vice versa*, such as a shield Argent with a lion gules, or a shield Gules with a lion Argent or Or. So one must make a coat of arms of colour and metal. For it cannot be of the two colours without metals, nor of two metals without colour. And therefore if it is Or or Argent it must have on it colour, or if the shield is colour it must have metal on it; and not colour on colour, nor metal on metal'.

That is a clear and a rather early mention of the rule.

The pursuivant then asks another question: 'Why then does the King of Jerusalem bear on a shield Argent a cross Or, which are two metals?'

The answer is: 'Because Godeffroy de Bouillon when he conquered Jerusalem assembled his council and they stated after good deliberation ... that he adopted these arms in memory of his noble conquest and that nobody else must bear two metals nor two colours for they would be false and bad achievements (car elles seroyent faulses et mal armoyées)'. My translation, understandably, is not literal but conforms to the sense of Sicille's archaic French.

Sicille wrote his treatise in the mid-fifteenth century, so how did he know that de Bouillon and his council had promulgated an heraldic law for all future times, centuries before heraldry even began to become fashionable?

Was the 'law' ever put in writing? And who has ever quoted such a document? Knowing something of the mentality and the level of formation of knights in the Middle Ages this seems most unlikely. Jerusalem was not conquered until 1099. Geoffrey was elected King and had already died in July 1100.

Geoffrey might well have had one or more golden crosses on his white tunic; or it is possible that they had this design on a flag and they liked it. At that time it was too early for it to have been an 'accepted exception'. Earlier parts of this book have shown how fantastic the imagination of heraldic authors could be (even King Solomon was declared to be a competent heraldist), but it is somehow understandable that later, when the rule was fixed, that the heralds should date it back to 1099, when no rule had even been intended to be established. By giving such antiquity to the previously unknown rule and its 'exception', it had become the more plausible.

Later, when heraldic ornaments became widespread and popular and in spite of the heralds' rule, many bearers of arms in every country of Europe have chosen Or and Argent, and no one could pretend that the results are ugly.

Certainly, while the vast majority of arms are of colour and metal, instances of the use of metal upon metal are quite numerous throughout the heraldic world, and even more numerous than certain combinations of metal with colour. Indeed, to secure visibility one has to choose a strong yellow which many of the heralds may call 'proper' in order, semantically, to save the rule.

GUSTAV A. SEYLER in his *Geschichte der Heraldik* (1889) of course mentions the rule: 'All his arms must have Or or Argent' (p.127). He admits, however, that 'unfortunately nothing can be found about the age of the rule' and continues:

'Johannes Rothe says precisely the same in his *Ritterspiegel* of 1386 which is the most ancient German armorial text book (*Wappenlehre*); a poem in Old German, which is the oldest written version of the rule – in practice always observed most severely – since the beginning of armory.'

'This law is not arbitary, but firmly founded in its perception. A coat of arms made in disregard of this law cannot accomplish an heraldic purpose because wrongly combined colours neutralise each other at a distance, some becoming indistinct, while well combined colours provide contrast and distinction one from the other'.

'Colours always appear in pairs; no coat of arms should have fewer, and without sufficient reason also not more than two colours' (p.126).

'The unique exception recognised by the science of armory are the arms of Jerusalem, which contain both metals. The

34

miscolouring of these arms really appears to belong to the oldest time' (p.128) In fact, of course, to pre-heraldic times.

Seyler then mentions a miniature of a Bavarian monk from 1188 representing Emperor Frederick I, the Redbeard, (1152-90) as a crusader with a shield on his back which is Argent, a cross Or. This would be an early medieval 'abusive' exception. Barbarossa Redbeard was not King of Jerusalem, thus the miniaturist did not think that gold on silver was wrong in 1188.

Seyler's observations are strict, but they do not offer any new aspect (apart from the evidence of this Bavarian monk). However, they obliged me to look for the original text of Johannes Rothe's *Ritterspiegel* – review for knights – (literally A Knight's Mirror Image) which Seyler calls the oldest written version of the rule, but in fact no rule is proclaimed in this text.

Johannes Rothe (b. 1360) mentioned as a priest in 1387, scholasticus of the Marienstift in Eisenach, chaplain of the Landgravine Anna, theologian, jurist and historian, a very cultured and well-read master, also called 'monachus Isnacensis', died on 5th May 1434. He wrote his 'Speculum' at the request of noblemen who were his friends. It is a poem of 4108 verses. It describes not only the ideal of a 'miles christianus', but also deals with the formation of knights, their virtues and vices, their religious duties and attachments, physical training, arms, and clothing and it gives directions for the improvement of their economical situation and even advice for warfare. Rothe severely blames gluttony, drunkenness, fornication, coursing and looting poor people as the activities that robber knights pursue.

Verses 595-615 and 639-650 concerning shields are of special interest for us. I doubt if Seyler had studied the text of the *Ritterspiegel* of which there exists only one MS. The edition by Neumann which I have before me, was edited in 1936, forty- seven years after Seyler's *Geschichte der Heraldik* . The text had been previously published in 1860 in a book about poems of the Middle Ages by Karl Bartsch who did not know who was the author of this poem.

Seyler dates it 1386, which seems to me to be impossible. I do not think that Rothe as a young priest of twenty-six would have dared to demean and blame princes and nobility as indeed he does, nor would he have possessed the vast experience on which the poem is based.

I think Neumann's dating, after 1412, is more correct. Rothe who was then over fifty, had acquired great respect and a considerable reputation and authority and his experience reached back into the XIVth century.

About heraldry, Rothe says:

593:     'Silbir adir golt di muszin lin
uf allin gewappintin schildin'

(Silver or gold must lay
on every armorial shield)

595: 'Wiz UND gel do vor ouch sin
an veldin adir an bildin'

(White AND yellow wherever they may
be colouring the field or the charge)

599: Weme deszir zcwoier varwe gebricht
adir weme daz velt ist grune,
Dem ist ez danne keyn wappin nicht'

(Whosoever lacks these two colours
or whose field is green
his is then not [a coat of] arms)

601: 'Welch schilt had gudir varwe zcwo
czu dem Velde UND zcu dem bilde'

(Whose shield has two good colours
on the field AND on the image [charge])

603: 'Ist er eyn guldin, den prise ich ho
vor di andirn gemeynen schilde'

(If it is golden, I value it high
before the other ordinary [common] shields)

605: 'Welchir abir had der farve dry
adir eyn ding genant unendelich
Dez wappin muszin swechis sy
sin adil gewest ist schendelich'

(But who has three colours
or something called unnoble
his arms must be weaker,
his nobility has been infamous)

610: 'Y mer eyn schilt der farve had
y mynner der wappin werdit geacht'

(The more colours a shield has
the less the arms are respected)

611: 'Y mynner bilde do habin stad
y edelicher sy sint gemacht'

(The fewer the charges are,
the nobler it is made)

6l3: 'Ist eyn schilt gehalbirit glich
di twernist adir di lenge'

(Is a shield halved [in] equal [parts]
per fess or per pale)

615: 'Dez bunt is veld do sunderlich
daz ander zcu bilde brenge'

(His coloured field particularly
should make the other part more apparent)

617: 'Wer danne di rechtin sitin had
von silbir adir von golde'

(Who then has the dexter side
of Argent or of Or)

620: 'Der had begangin di bestin tad
an dez konigis solde'

(This [one] has done the best deed
in the king's service)

In the following verses Rothe talks about birds, wild or tame animals, bars of different colours and other charges, but he does NOT point out any colour by name (as Gules, Azure or Sable).

With verse 639 he comes back to tinctures:

'Si edilir gar sere di schilde
sint sy mit golde umleid'

(The nobler are the shields
if they are surrounded with gold)

641: 'Vel edilir ist eyn gulden veld
danne eyn guldin bilde'
(Much nobler is a golden field
than a golden charge)

In the translations I have had to change the syntactical order in an attempt to make them more fluent and understandable. (Translating to modern German would compel me to do so as well.)

643: Daz silbir had daz selbe geld
wanne man di ere gancz hilde'

(Silver has the same value
when one holds the honour unblemished)

645: 'Ab eyn man mit manheit ader mit list
irwerbit der ritter ordin'

(Whether a man with manfulness or with cunning acquired the knightly status)

647: 'Daz silbir daz in sime schild ist
ist darumme nicht guldin wordin'

(the silver that is on his shield
has therefore not become golden*)

651: 'Di gele farwe sal vor daz gold sin
di betudit ez mit er craft'

(Yellow colour stands for gold
this it signifies with vigour)

* Does Rothe want to say that if a man bears gold on his shield it does not necessarily mean that he is a knight? We give Rothe's full text about colours just to show that he does not mention the rule

After verse 653 Rothe talks again about animals, birds, fishes, flowers, leaves, trees, stripes and other heraldic symbols, but never indicates colours.

671: 'Alt adil kan ez gemeldin
ab ez zcwo farve begriffit'

(It can proclaim ancient nobility
if it includes two colours)

The poem does not say any more about colours. Or and Argent, (yellow and white) are called colours. The only other colour mentioned is green; and green is, curiously, disqualified by Rothe as an armorial colour. As we have seen, there is no mention of a rule or any kind of incompatibility. Rothe does not mention the exception for the King of Jerusalem. All that he says in this context is: 'Argent or Or must be on every shield. Yellow AND white can be on the field and/or on the charge. When these two colours are wanting then it is not [a coat of] arms.'

Seyler has deduced much more from the text than actually appears in the *Ritterspiegel*, as we can see.

We may conclude, therefore, that Rothe knew nothing about any rule obliging us to believe the story of Geoffrey de Bouillon's council decreeing only one permitted exception for all time. It is, however, clear that Rothe considered it necessary that Or or Argent should appear on every shield. This practice was at his time, and certainly before, the prevailing thinking about noble arms. But Rothe does not distinguish between colours and metals, and he never uses the word 'metal': the only colour he mentions is green, which is disqualified by him. Indeed, green does not often appear in early German heraldry (Uradel heraldry).

JOHANNES DE BADO AUREO's (the Latin version of John of Guildford's) *Tractatus de Armis* is the oldest known heraldic treatise written in England. It is based, as he tells us, on the work of his 'most excellent teacher Master Franciscus de Foveis', a Frenchman who has never been identified.

Bado's *Tractatus* was completed shortly after 1394 and was eventually published in 1654 by Edoardus Bissaeus (Sir Edward Bysshe) and in 1943 by Evan John Jones.

His colour-philosophy is long and fanciful like that of many later heraldists, and it is based upon that of Bartolus de Saxoferrato who, however, is more sober and concise. Bado's concern is to state which colour is the most noble (white), and which the least reputable, (black).

Bartolus's order is different. He begins with Gules, Azure and White, as we shall see later.

I have already commented on what we think about mixtures of black and white becoming (contrary to science) fine heraldic colours.

For Bado, Or is the most noble, most splendid and most precious metal, but as a colour it is not of as high a value as white. All these considerations are not important for our purpose and practically of no interest for an heraldic painter of our time.

Yet what must be said is that, in all this discursive and verbose treatise about colours, no mention is made about the metal or the colour rule, nor about any incompatibility. In Bysshe's edition we have the following illustrations:

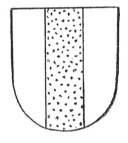
p. 37
non blazoned

p. 26
De argento
cum sua cruce
florida
(he does not
say more)

p. 40
de Auro
cum una fissura
ingradata
de argento

THE DEAN TRACT: Ruth J. Dean, *An Early Treatise on Heraldry in Anglo-Norman* (c. 1382, but thought by some to be earlier).

'The University Library of Cambridge preserves a number of manuscripts in Latin, English and Anglo-Norman which appear to have been compiled for the use of households' about different topics of legal and economic import.

One such miscellany is contained in MS Ee. 4.20. 'One Anglo-Norman work of this codex is a treatise on heraldry entitled *De Heraudie*' (Dean, p. 22).

The volume was compiled at St Albans over a period of several years beginning in 1382 (that is after Matthew Paris's time). Ruth Dean, who is interested in the Anglo-Norman language rather than in heraldry, examines (pp. 25-29) f.160v of the MS 'with the marginal title: Descriptio armorum sive scutorum diversorum in Gallicis' and gives the original text of a poem of 144 verses which contains a kind of armorial mentioning thirty-four coats of arms, preceded and mixed with some heraldic theses on such subjects as colours, furs, animals and other charges.

Occasionally, there is some personal comment, as when the author reports a dispute among heralds about the arms of Mortimer or criticizes the charging of gold on silver.

The only verses of the poem that are of particular interest in our context are 79 and 80: 'Le Roy de Jerusalem porte l'escu d'argent croislee d'or a une croise potente d'or. Et si avient malement* couleur d'or en argent', without any other comment. This is, maybe, the earliest documented statement that Or on Argent was considered an unfit combination. It is declared bad, but not 'the only admitted exception'; neither is the later invented story mentioned about Geoffroy de Bouillon being advised by the committee of his fellow combatants to use these colours to commemorate the glorious victory of the Crusaders, nor that it should be the only tolerated break of a rule. In 1100 this rule simply did not exist. It simply tells us that by the end of the fourteenth century metal on metal was considered bad: 'si avient malement couleur d'or en argent'.

Matthew Paris (+1259) mentions the arms of Jerusalem many times without finding them irregular. He blazons them differently. The arms (or flag) of Geoffrey de Bouillon when he relates his death (+1100) are: Or a cross Argent, equally for Balduin I succeeding (1100), for Fulk (+1143) and for Henry de Champagne (+1197). 'Crusuly' appears the first time for John de Brienne (+1237): 'Scutum aureum crux alba cum multis crucibus albis' (MP II 1).

BARTOLUS DE SAXOFERRATO (+1359): The first clear and terse treatise on heraldry is the *Tractatus de Insigniis et Armis* written by this famous jurist in 1350 and published after his death by his son-in-law Niccolo Alessandro, himself a Doctor of Law.

It is a systematic treatise preceded by a list of thirty-three questions and their answers. The first twelve topics concern juridical principles connected with the granting, the assumption, the bearing and the inheritance of insignia and arms.

With point 13, Bartolous begins giving practical heraldic guidlines: how arms must be painted, placed and borne, in which position animals must be placed upon shields and banners, how animals, such as lions, bears, horses, lambs, etc. should be designed and in which poise and attitude they should appear. Personally, I must admit to having been guided by Bartolous' standards ever since I first started painting arms.

From points 23-27, Bartolus writes clearly and distinctly about heraldic colours and in which order they should be arranged. Or is the most noble colour. It represents the sun. Nothing is more noble than light. The red colour represents fire and that is noble. Azure is the third colour, it represents the air.

The colour white is more noble than black, and black is the lowest. Bartolus was interested in heraldry and most competent, and he is the first master who looks beyond juridical principles to offer guidelines for heraldic art and style. He was for a short time a Privy Councillor. He collaborated in the preparation of the Golden Bull issued in 1356, and he was given arms for himself and his family by Emperor Charles IV: Or, a double-tailed lion Gules.

He must have heard about the colour and metal rule had it existed, but he does not mention it, though talking very precisely about heraldic tinctures, their rank and placement upon banners and shields. How could he with his juridical mind overlook such an important rule if it were common practice at his time? Can we suggest that he did not find it important, nor really so strictly practised as some pretend? It is inconceivable to imagine that he had forgotten it or that he would not have been quick to condemn 'false' arms? I must conclude that in the early XIVth century it was not general knowledge that Geoffrey de Bouillon and his councillors had decreed an heraldic law for all future time, otherwise Bartolus de Saxoferrato in Italy and Johannes de Bado Aureo in England could not have ignored it.

Yet, although later heraldists would have us believe that they knew of this previously unknown decree, there are many earlier instances of (so-called) breaches of the Or and Argent rule before it was even invented.

CONCLUSION

To conclude we have to say: the first time (as far as I know) that we find Or and Argent arms being criticized is in the Dean Tract (1382). The arms of the King of Jerusalem are declared bad. Nothing more.

The first heraldist who mentions the Jerusalem story, telling us that Geoffrey de Bouillon was advised by the princes in his company that he should bear arms different from his less exalted companions, is presented to us in the Argentaye Tract by an anonymous author in 1412.

Now let us ask: who has ever seen even one of the arms of any of those less exalted princes painted or described?

Johannes de Bado Aureo (1394) and Bartolus de Saxoferrato (1350) knew nothing of the Jerusalem decision nor about an obligatory rule against metal on metal.

It is, however, certain that arms with metal on metal and colour on colour are, for obvious reasons, less frequent than metal with colour arms, but all the same we find a considerable number of Or and Argent arms before and after the fourteenth century.

What more can we say? To over-emphasize our point we may draw attention to the superabundance of instances to be found in Rolland's Illustrations to Rietstap's Armorial Général. In the six volumes we find more than 1500 Or and Argent shields from all over Europe of which we show only a small number of typical examples.

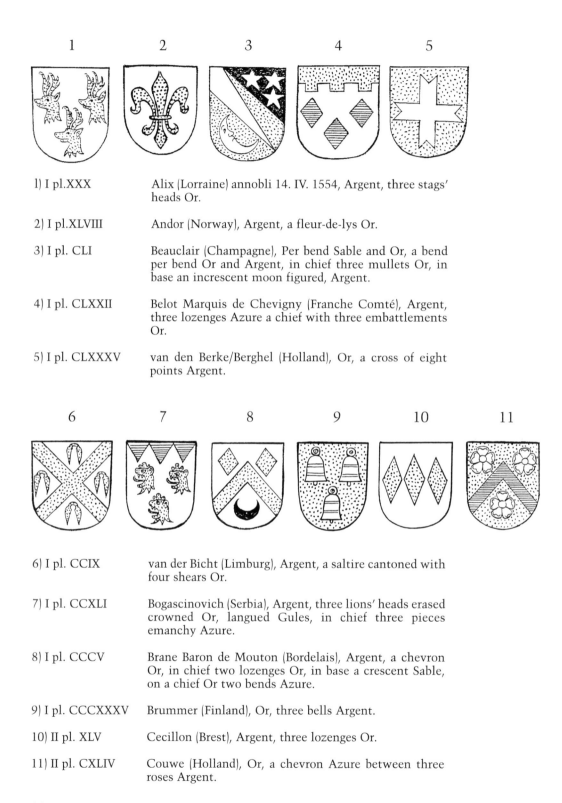

1) I pl.XXX   Alix (Lorraine) annobli 14. IV. 1554, Argent, three stags' heads Or.

2) I pl.XLVIII   Andor (Norway), Argent, a fleur-de-lys Or.

3) I pl. CLI   Beauclair (Champagne), Per bend Sable and Or, a bend per bend Or and Argent, in chief three mullets Or, in base an increscent moon figured, Argent.

4) I pl. CLXXII   Belot Marquis de Chevigny (Franche Comté), Argent, three lozenges Azure a chief with three embattlements Or.

5) I pl. CLXXXV   van den Berke/Berghel (Holland), Or, a cross of eight points Argent.

6) I pl. CCIX   van der Bicht (Limburg), Argent, a saltire cantoned with four shears Or.

7) I pl. CCXLI   Bogascinovich (Serbia), Argent, three lions' heads erased crowned Or, langued Gules, in chief three pieces emanchy Azure.

8) I pl. CCCV   Brane Baron de Mouton (Bordelais), Argent, a chevron Or, in chief two lozenges Or, in base a crescent Sable, on a chief Or two bends Azure.

9) I pl. CCCXXXV   Brummer (Finland), Or, three bells Argent.

10) II pl. XLV   Cecillon (Brest), Argent, three lozenges Or.

11) II pl. CXLIV   Couwe (Holland), Or, a chevron Azure between three roses Argent.

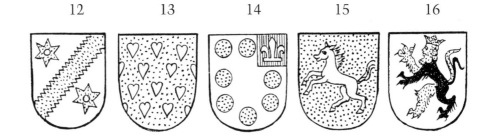

12) II pl. CLXX   Chaufour (Normandy), Argent, a bend indented between two pierced mullets Or.

13) II pl. CLXIII   Curcuas (Greece), Or semée of hearts Argent.

14) II pl. CLXXXI   Baron Davillier (France), Argent, an orle of eight bezants and on a sinister canton Gules a fleur-de-lys couped Argent.

15) II pl. CCCIII   Farkas de Nagy-Joka (Hungary), Or, a horse salient Argent.

16) II pl. CCCLXXIII   Funck de Senftenau (Styria), Argent, a lion rampant guardant Sable crowned Or, with a human face Or, the right gamb and the right paw Or, (double) queued (Or &) Sable.

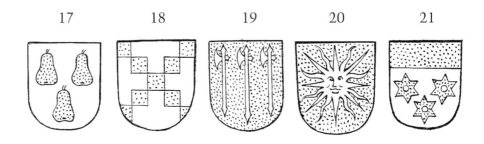

17) III pl. VI   le Gal de estrevenec (Brittany), Argent, three pears Or.

18) III pl. XV   Gardisseul (Brittany), Argent, a saltire of nine lozenges conjoined Or.

19) IV pl. LII   Lesmabon (Brittany), Or, three halberds palewise in fess Argent.

20) V pl. CLIII   Rhadino (Greece) Or, a sun Argent.

21) VI pl.LVII   Tubières de Levis (Ile-de-France), Argent, three stars of six points pierced and a chief Or.

Moreover, for those who think and write that the Continent is mostly responsible for breaches of the sacred rule we show the fine episcopal arms of Bath and Wells and of Lichfield.

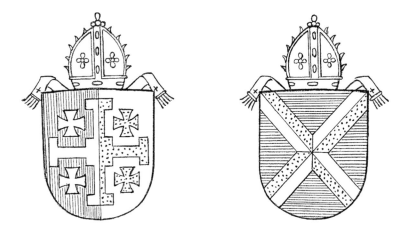

And let us also remind our friends that on the external north side of the Council Chamber of Winchester, one of the former capitals of England, we can see the arms of Norman knights and barons who assisted in building the city after its destruction at the Conquest (1066-1080). These years were, of course, pre-heraldic, but the arms we see are those of the same families as used after 1200. Six of these eighteen shields show Or/Argent combinations and four colour on colour!

THE COLOUR PLATES

Plate I

Plate I

1-4. We first show four shields from pre- or proto-heraldic times. Four shields from the famous tapestry of BAYEUX representing the Battle of Hastings (1066).

Next we quote from *Aspilogia II* (A II) & from Cecil Humphery-Smith's *Anglo-Norman Armory* (A-N) and *Anglo-Norman Armory Two, an Ordinary of Thirteenth-Century Armorials* (AN II).

5. Matthew Paris; (MP III/47) writes: 'De miserabili morte comitis GILEBERTI MARESCALLI' showing his arms in colour: Per pale Or and Vert, a lion rampant Argent (over all). (See A II plate I (d)). The shield is reversed because he is relating the story of Gilbert's death at the tournament of Hertford (1241). (A II, p.67) (William Marshal, who died 1219, bore: Per pale Or and Vert, a lion rampant Gules, which would be against the colour rule (A II, p. 62).

6. HUGH WAKE died also in 1241. His arms, also reversed, are: Or, two bars Gules and in chief three roundels Argent. (MP III n. 50, A II , p. 68).

7. Another instance proving that Matthew Paris did not object to Gold on Silver is: Scutum REGIS HISPANIAE: 'campus de gules castrum de auro, campus de argento leo de auro [sic]'. These are the arms of Alphonso X, The Wise, King of Castile and Leon (1254-84): Quarterly, 1 and 4: Gules, a triple towered castle Or; 2 & 3, Argent, a lion rampant Or. (MP IV, n. 83; A II, p. 74). Later, the colouring of Leon was different, but in the 1250s MP did not hesitate blazoning it Or upon Argent.

8. The Empire: MANFRED OF APULIA was created King in 1254 and MP VI/9 blazons and paints his arms: 'Or, a double [-headed] eagle Sable and over all a fess Argent. (MP VI, n. 9, A II p. 76).

9. In Glover's Roll, no. 32, A II, p. 121, we have the arms of ROGER MORTIMER of Wigmore (+1282). He bore: 'bende a chief pale a corneres geronne [d'or et d'azur] ove un escucheon [d'argent]'. (His son, Sir Edmund Mortimer of Wigmore, baron 1295, bore as did his father Roger: Barry of six Or and Azure on a chief of the first three palets Or between two esquires based of the second, overall an inescucheon Argent.' (cf. Foster p. 143 and Jones, Plate IX a).*

* Ruth Dean in *An Early Treatise on Heraldry in Anglo-Norman*, p. 23, writes: The author reports a dispute about the arms of Mortimer criticising the charging of gold.

10. Glover's Roll gives the arms of WILLIAM LA ZOUCHE of Marston: 'd'argent besante d'or'. 'That, no doubt is what was in the 1253 manuscript. Glover, however has tricked it 'b' (i.e. azure)'. (Why has he tricked it and why 'b' instead of Azure like the lines below?) (A II . no . 86, p. 131).

11. The arms of JOHN DE CLERE in Cecil Humphery-Smith's *Anglo-Norman Armory* (p. 29) are blazoned: Argent, a fess diapered Or (Matthew de Clere is mentioned 1172; John was an illegitimate son of Richard, Duke of Normandy).

12. Also in *Anglo-Norman Armory* the arms of CREVE-COEUR (Artois) are blazoned: Argent, three chevrons Or (p. 36 & p. 13) 'Crevecoeur appearing on a deed prior to King Richard I [1198/99].'

13. ROBERT PIERPOINT's arms are blazoned: Argent, a lion rampant Sable langued Gules surmounted by a bendlet Or. (Here the bendlet is designed a little too large) (AN II, p. 67) (1308).

14. GILES PLAYS's arms are: Per pale Or and Gules, a lion passant guardant Argent (AN II, p. 91. Giles Plays, Baron at 1297).

15. ALAN FRERE, (c. 1285) bore: Argent, two bends Or (AN II, p. 181) .

16. WILLIAM RYE (c. 1310) bore: Argent (?), six crescents Or (AN II, p. 308). Why this question mark? Why should there be doubt when there are so many similar instances?

For more examples from the Middle Ages of Or/Argent arms see AN II.

P. 34, Kingsmede, Walter (1312); p.36, Mortimer, Henry (1285); p. 70, Breves, William (1298); p.92, Bigod, Ralph (1285); p. 94, Cornwall, Edmund (1312); p.99, Tirrel, Roger (1304); p. 107, Strange, Hamon (1308); p. 124, Box, Henry (1312); p. 202, Grandone, John (1312); p. 381, Baudris, Bocars (1530).

In Glover's Roll, A II. 131, p.140, we find the arms of ROGER DE HUNTINGFIELD (+1257): or a fess Gules in chief three roundels Argent'.

In Walford's Roll we have the arms of JOHN DE MONEMUTH: 'd'or a iii cheverons de gules a une fesse d'argent'. (A II, p.185, n.88) see also plate XI/8.

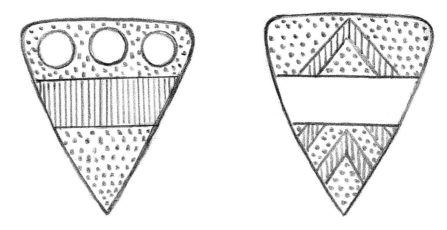

MP VIII, n.9, speaking of the siege of Lincoln by King Louis and the Barons in 1217, Paris describes the banner of Lincoln Castle: Or, three lions passant guardant Argent (alternatively with two gemel bars) and MP VIII, n.12, relating the capture of Bedford Castle 1224 blazons the banner of the castle also: Or, three lions guardant Argent (A II, p.81).

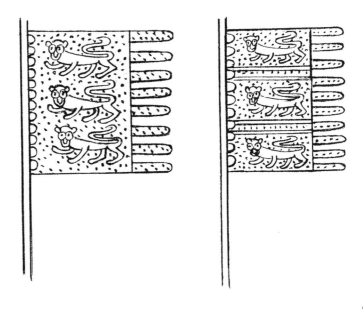

Plate II Plate II

1. DE SAISSET, Seigneur de Saint-Agnan: 'd'azur à la gerbe d'or au chef d'argent chargé de 3 étoiles d'or. Guillaume de Saisset se marie en 1202. Raymond de Saisset et Gentille de Ricaud sont parents de Bernard de Saisset (1232-1311) qui en 1267 devint Abbé de Saint-Antonin de Pamiers, et en 1295 premier évêque de Pamiers (diocèse érigé par Boniface VIII). Comme évêque de Parmiers Bernard de Saisset "avait au poing l'épée plutôt que la crosse".' See: Comte Georges de Morant, *Armorial Français*, p. 292 and Mgr. J. M. Vidal's *Histoire de l'évêques de Pamiers*).

2. The present arms of the Kingdom of Sweden include the arms of the House of FOLKUNGA: Azure, three bends sinister wavy Argent, a lion rampant Or overall. BIRGER JARL, Regent of Sweden, 1250-66, and:-

3. The arms of the House of VASA. Niels Vasa (+1378), Christian Vasa (+1442), John Vasa (+1477): Per bend Azure Argent and Gules, a vase Or overall, see Louda and Maclagan *Lines of Succession*, table 26/27.

4. At the time when Bosnia was part of the Austro-Hungarian Empire, 1878-1918, the arms of Bosnia were: Or, a harnessed dexter arm gules issuing from a sinister cloud Argent holding a sword of the same. The reason for this was that arms of STEVEN OSTORIA, King of Bosnia (+1418) were: Or, an arm Gules holding a sword Argent (without the cloud). See: Louda and Maclagan, table 144, and *Die Österreichisch-Ungarische Monarchie in Wort und Bild*, K. & K. Hof-und Staatsdruckerei Wien 1901, p. 276.

5. EDNYFED FYCHAN (+1246) bore: 'Gold three helms silver and a chevron of the same colour of silver' (see Siddons: *The Development of Welsh Heraldry*, p. 233) .

6. JEAN D'AVENCHY, Seigneur du dit lieu (1390), bore: 'parti d'argent et de gueules à la cotice d'or brochant sur le tout'. (See: de Foras, *Armorial de Savoie* I, p. 80).

7. AMÉDÉ DE GILLY, Seigneur de Villamaron (1240): 'd'or à trois fasces de gueules à la bande d'argent chargée de trois merlettes de sable brochant sur le tout' (de Foras II, p.112).

8. AIMON DE LUGRIN, chevalier 1247: 'fascé d'or et d'azur à la cotice ondée d'argent' (de Foras III, p. 295).

9. PELARD, Seigneur du Nogret, etc: 'd'azur à deux chevrons entrelacés en sautoir, celui du chef renversé d'or l'autre d'argent, cantonnés de quatre étoiles à 7 & à 8 rais. Louis Pélard épouse à Lausanne en 1392 Pernette d'Arlos de Genève' (de Foras IV, p. 357).

10. ROBERT DE BILLEMORE bore at the second Dunstable Tournament in 1334: Argent a bend Gules a bordure engrailed Or. (Foster: *Some Feudal Coats of Arms*, p. 21, and Chesshyre & Woodcock: *Dictionary of British Arms*, p. 394).

11. ROBERT BOURCHIER bore at the second Dunstable Tournament in 1334: Argent, a cross engailed Or. (Foster, p. 28).

12. Sir Richard LEIGHTON (1313) bore: Quarterly per fess indented Or and Gules, over all a bendlet Argent (Foster, p.126).

13. Sir Nichol DE LONGFORD bore at the Battle of Borrowbridge (1322): Paly of six Or and Gules, a bend Argent (Foster, p. 124).

14. COLLINS ROLL (ca. 1295) Barry Or and Argent, a bend Gules (Chesshyre & Woodcock: *Dictionary of British Arms*, p. 328).

15. SIMON, Seigneur de Champigny et de la Rochette, Conseiller au Parlement de Paris 1435: 'd'or à une fasce de gueules (d'argent) accompagnée en chef de deux glands d'argent en pointe d'une coquille d'argent' (d'Hozier, VI. 225).

16. RANBLY de Laissardière (Bourgogne 1550): 'd'argent à un tremble d'or' (d'Hozier, VII. 344).

17. DE SÉGLA (Languedoc, anobli en 1596): 'd'argent à trois épis de seigle d'or' (d'Hozier, VI. 195).

18. John CHAMPAYN, Kent Gentry, ca. 1490 Cotton MS: Argent, two bars wavy Or [sic] (Chesshyre & Woodcock, p. 25).

19. The Earl of Shrewsbury: Argent a lion and border engrailed Or, (Bradfer-Lawrence Roll 1445/46, Chesshyre & Woodcock, p. 241 (no *sic*, but it would deserve *sics*!)). I know

that elsewhere it is blazoned Gules but here it is *sic*. That at least means that one did not always care over much about the rule.

20. Le COMTE DOUGLAS, Stodart, 1370: Argent, a bend Or between seven crosslets Azure (Chesshyre & Woodcock, p. 383).

21. Sir John TOCHET: Argent, guty Or a lion Sable. (Calveley's book, *Becket's Murderers* Roll c. 1350, (Chesshyre & Woodcock, p. 153).

22. Jacques d'Armagnac, Duc de Nemours (1433-77), is believed to have 'compiled a list of names and arms of 150 knights of the Arthurian Round Table'. 'BREUNOR OF THE CASTLE PLUERE: Quarterly Or and Sable, over all a fountain Argent gushing water downwards from a rectangular opening'. Of course, these arms are invented, but prove that the Duc de Nemours did not mind Argent upon Or (see Scott-Giles in *The Coat of Arms*, VIII, 1965, p. 336).

23. Vulson, chevalier Sieur de la Colombière also gives names and arms of the knights of the Round Table in his *Theatre d'honneur* (1648): p. 143 he says 'BUSTERIN LE GRAND, portoit d'or deux clefs d'argent posées en pal et adossées; ces armes sont à enquérir, pource qu'elles sont de métal sur métal qui est une fausseté selon la science des armoiries; à moins qu'il y ait un sujet et raison importante pour permettre cette irrégularité.' Why then does he not enquire?

24. De MAUREL (Languedoc, preuves de 1540) 'MARQUIS D'ARAGON, Seigneur de Raissac porte d'argent au chevron d'or accompagné de trois molettes d'or' (d'Hozier, V, 21).

25. The DUQUES DE AHUMADA : 1 & 4, de plata una cruz do mismo filetada de sable; 2 & 3, de oro 5 estrelas de plata (Piferer nr. 1965, Tomo V, lamina 5).

26. GUYOT DE MALSEIGNE ET DE MAICHE (Franche Comté) filiation prouvée de 1574, Baron de Malseigne, titré Marquis de la Maiche porte 'd'or au chevron d'argent accompagné de trois roses du même, deux en chef et une en pointe' (d'Hozier, IV, 263).

Plate III
Plate III

STODART, R.R., *Scottish Arms, being a collection of Armorial Bearings A.D. 1370-1678 Reproduced in Facsimile from Contemporary Manuscripts.* Edinburgh, 1881. They are not blazoned but clearly coloured as we reproduce them.

1. p.C: Le seigneur Patrick
2. p.14: Wardhus of Varostoune
3. p.21: Balfour of Kirktoune
4. p.49: Froyst
5. p.51: Fouler
6. p.52: Trollop (may be meant as proper, a verbal difference)
7. p.61: Fynnyk
8. p.63: Hislop (same as 6)
9. p.64: Villumer
10. p.67: Craik
11. p.68: Horne
12. p.95: Grant Ao 1492, Sir James Balfour's MS
13. p.99: Bowle
14. p.101: Boyle
15. p.104: Poyet of Auchinheirsseir
16. p.115 Mc aula of Arncapelle

There are more examples of gold with silver abutting in this same manuscript:

p.6; Crulx de Bediton;

p.7; James Keith of Tilligonic;

p.23; The Lord of Pewes-Maccloyd, VIII;

p.37; The Lord Lewis;

p.50; STEWART ERLE ARRAN quarterings 8 & 14 (see plate XXIV n.6.);

p.95; Corre of Elwood Olim, 1420;

p.97; James Keith of Tilligonie;

p.98; Donald McDonald of Maydert;

p.147; Langton of Langton.

Plate IV Plate IV

The *Zürich Roll of Arms* is an heraldic monument of the XIVth century. The facsimile edition, Orell Füssli, Zürich and Leipsig, MCMXXX, provides us with fifteen Or/Argént examples, twelve of which are reproduced here:

1. n.124: SCHWANDEGG: Argent, a steinbock Sable within a bordure Or. Burchart von Schwandegg (Swandeg), noble muster captain of the Counts of Habsburg (1266).

2. n.150: SCHIENEN: Azure, on a star of eight points a triple mount Argent. Hiltiboldus de Shiniin, Canon of Constance (1211).

3. n.190: CASTEL: Per pale Or and Argent, a lion passant guardant Gules. Ulrich de Castello, ministerialis ecclesie Constantiensis (1170).

4. n.226: BURGBERG: Quarterly Argent and Gules, in the first quarter a castle [Burg] with two towers Or on a mount Vert. Hartman de Burcberc, vassal of Reichenau Abbey (1182).

5. n.284: OBERRIEDEN: Argent, a boat Sable with two oars Or. Burcardus de Obirriedin, Ministeriale of the see of Constance (1134/37).

6. n.286: SALENSTEIN: Per pale Or and Argent, a hill of ten peaks Azure. Adelbertus de Salestein (1094); Henricus & Habardus de Salestein, Canons of Constance, (1158).

7. n.387: RAMUNGS: Per pale Argent and Or, a boar's head and neck couped Gules bristled Argent. Dietrich von Ramungs, Ritter (knight) (1363).

8. n.447: FACKELSTEIN: Argent, a torch [Fackel] in pale Or flaming Gules. Vassals of the Bishops of Chur; Ulrich von Fackelstein, arbitrator (1365).

9. n.484: no name: Per fess Argent and Or, a stag's attire Sable.

10. n.499: ISENBURG: Per pale Argent and Sable, an escarbuncle Or (over all). Wernherus de Ysenburg, miles (1235-1262).

11. n.556: WALDSTRASS: Or, a fess nebuly Argent and Azure. Dietrich an der Waltstras, his castle on the road from Rottweil to Neukirch (1200)

Plate V

12 n.551: BURLADINGEN: Or, a bird Argent with claws and a bordure Gules. Landolt von Burladingen (1184/89) monk in the Abbey of Reichenau, Gotfridus vir nobilis de Burladingen (1283).

Plate V

L'armorial du Héraut Gelre 1370-1395, Bruxelles, BR MS 15653-56, illustrated edition by Jan van Helmont, Leuven, 1992, (publié et annoté par Paul Adam-Even dans Archives Héraldiques Suisses 1961-68 qui l'appelle "un des chefs-d'oeuvres de l'art héraldique").

Among 1755 arms we find several examples of Or and Argent and we reproduce just fifteen:

1. 367: DIE ERE V. ANGELUSE: d'or semis de pièces enlevées en angle de gueules, accostées de grelots d'argent.

2. 523: HER TIBIER: coupé crenelé d'argent et de gueules au lion issuant d'or lampassé de gueules

3. 1595: H. HENRIJC v. HUERDE: d'or au chien ravissant coupé de sable et d'argent langué de gueules.

4. 296: Dye BISSCOP V. HILDENES HEYM Gerard v.d. Berge (1365-1398): parti d'or et de gueules, sur le tout un écu d'argent au vol abaissé de sable lié d'or.

5. 725: Die Maerscale, Karl Ulfsson (1363-1407): taillé de gueules et d'argent au lion brochant d'or.

6. 1297: DIE GREVE v. CLEVE Cleves Adolph I de la Marck (1368-1395): de gueules à l'écusson d'argent au rais d'escarboucle fleurdelisé d'or brochant.

7. 1733: He. v. AVELYNS: d'argent au lion de gueules lampassé d'azure à la bordure endentée d'or.

8. 84: HER MATHYS V. D. SPIEGEL: de gueules à trois miroirs d'argent cerclés d'or.

9. 104: HER CRAS V. OUDENDORP (Kratz v. Oudendorf: d'argent à l'écusson de gueules accompagné d'un annelet d'or. (The little gold ring is free in the dexter chief and not in a canton).

10. 224: RAMSDORF: d'argent une fourche de bois d'or.

Plate VI

11. 234: STAEL – veneur de Basse Bavière: parti de gueules et d'or à la pile d'argent sur le tout.

12. 244: Die van Konixte (Königstein): tranché de sable et d'or une barre d'argent sur l'or.

13. 368: H. WILLEM BOUTEONT: Bouttemont en Normandie: de sable à trois besants d'or une étoile d'argent sur le premier.

14. 1427: Die NEGENDANC (Negendank): d'argent embrassé à dextre en chef d'or, en pointe de gueules.

15. 1479 DIE HERTOGE v. VYNEGEN: palé d'argent et d'azur à la fasce d'or brochant (the Doge Antonio Montalto of Genoa, 1383, has the same arms).

Plate VI

In Italy the arms with Or and Argent together are very frequent. The *Elenco Storico Della Nobiltà Italiana*, a colour illustrated edition of the S.M. Order of Malta (ca.1960) shows more than 300 instances. This list is not at all historic, it gives no dates.

The Marchese Spreti in his *Enciclopeda Storico-Nobiliare Italiana* mentions more than 80 instances of arms with combinations of Or and Argent.

We prefer, however, to show instances from the famous *Armoriale Trivulziano*. It was formerly owned by the Marquesses Trivulzio and now by the City of Milan, as Codice 1390. It is kept in the Castello Sforzesco.

This armorial has been blazoned by Alberto to Crescentini between 1959 and 1966 in the *Rivista Araldica* published in Rome by the Accademia del Collegio Araldico (founded by Pope Pius IX).

The order is not strictly alphabetical and the number of the page is often not given nor can it be easily read. I therefore visited the Sforza Castle to study Codex 1390. I counted more than 200 shields in which Or and Argent appear together. I have taken copies, and on this plate I have reproduced, in the style of Codex 1390, sixteen instances in Crescentini's order.

1. 41/IV, de APLANO: d'argento all'aquila con ali abbassate

di rosso, accompagnata in capo da due stelle (8 punte) d'oro. [Argent, an eagle Gules in chief two estoiles Or].

2. 47/I, de ARONA: d'argento una stella (8 punte) d'oro posta tra due semivoli addossati e rivolti di nero. [Argent, an estoile of eight points Or between two eagle wings Sable].

3. 74/VIII, di BANFI: d'oro all'aquila fasciata d'azzuro e d'argento armata, imbeccata e linguata di rosso. [Or, an eagle barry of five Azure and Argent].

4. 70/1, de BALMISERIS: d'oro alla banda inferiormente dentata d'argento, accompagnata da tre trifogli il gambo formante un anello verdi. [Or, a bend indented on the lower side Argent between three trefoils the stalks forming a circle Vert].

5. 118/VI, da CARUAZO: troncato d'oro e di rosso al leone d'argento linguato di rosso attraversante. [Per fess Or and Gules, a lion rampant Argent overall].

6. 91/II, de CAVRATE: d'argento due bastoni gigliati di oro posti in croce di S. Andrea, accompagnati in capo da una torre di rosso aperta e finestrata del campo. [Argent, two sceptres in saltire Or, in chief a tower Gules].

7. 99/VII, de CERMENIAGA: d'oro al castello d'argento torricellato di due pezzi, aperto e finestrato del campo, fondato sulla campagna di verde, accompagnata da due arbusti moventi dal campo cimato ciascuno da un fiore a cinque fogli d'argento bottonato d'oro; il castello sostenente un aquila nera, le zampe sulle due torri. [Or, issuant from the base between two plants Vert with a flower Argent, a double towered castle Argent in chief an eagle displayed Sable its claws grasping the two towers].

8. 100/II, de CERNISIO: d'argento al lupo rapace d'oro; col capo dell'Impero. [Argent, a wolf rampant Or, on a chief Or an eagle displayed Sable, called in Italy the chief of the Empire].

9. 232/I, de MOLA: d'argento ai due leoni affrontati /controrampanti d'oro, linguati ed immaschiti di rosso tenenti una mola del campo. [Argent, two lions rampant respecting each other Or holding a mill-stone of the field – Crescenti does not blazon the five bezants over the mill-stone].

10. 222/I, de MOMBRETO: palato d'oro e di rosso alla torre d'argento, aperta e finestrata del campo attraversente [paly of six Or and Gules, a tower Argent over all].

11. 249/V, de NAVA: d'argento alla barca d'oro fluttuante su un mare di verde scuro. [Argent, a bark Or flotant on a bluish sea].

12. 249/VI, de NIGRI: in quartato d'oro e di verde alla stella (sei punte) d'argento attraversante. [Quarterly Or and Vert, a star of six points Argent over all].

13. 288/II, da PALAZZOLO: d'oro una torre di due piani d'argento, al destrocherio uscente della finestra del primo piano, vestito di rosso, impugnante un remo (d'argento) posto in banda; col capo dell'Impero. [Or, a tower of two levels Argent Gules vested dexter arm issuing from a window holding an oar Argent; the chief of the Empire].

14. 275/V, de PARNTERIS: bandato d'oro e d'argento, le bende d'argento caricate la prime e la terza di uno stella, la seconda di un crescente del primo. [Bendy of six Argent and Or, the first and third pieces Argent charged with a star of six points the second with a crescent all Or].

15. 286/VI, de PONTREMOLO: d'argento al semivolo abbassato d'oro trafitto da una freccia posta in fascia la punta a destra d'argento: [Argent, a wing inverted Or pierced fesswise by an arrow Argent feathered Gules].

16. 321/VIII, di SANTO VITTORE: troncato merlato d'argento e d'oro, col capo troncato di rosso e di nero. [Per fess embattled Argent and Or, a chief per fess Gules and Sable].

Here we wish to mention another fine Italian XVth century armorial of the noble families of the City and ancient Diocese of Como, called *Codice Carpani* published by Carlo Maspoli in Lugano (Switzerland) in 1973. It contains forty-five Or/Argent arms of which we show three.

1. DE BRESANIS c. 16. v.e: Or, a lion sable the rear part of the dexter leg and the tail Argent.

2. DE BRENTANIS c.18.r.: Argent, a "brenta" [back bucket/ basket] Or within a border compony Argent and Gules.

3. DE VACHARIS c.72.v.a.: Argent, a cow passant Gules carrying a fleur-de-lis Or on its back.

Plate VII

Plate VII

Ulrich von Richenthal's *Das Concilium* Chronicle of the Council of Constance (1414-18) Facsimile edition 1936 is lavishly illustrated with coats of arms of participators from many countries, amongst them sixty examples of Or upon Argent.

1. p.XVIII: HANS HAGEN, Bailiff: Argent, issuing from a bend a demi fleur-de-lis Or (towards the sinister).

2. p.XLII: LAMPERTUS DE STIPITE, Doctor in Theologia: Argent, three wolves passant in pale Or.

3. p.CLIIII: Nicolaus SCHRANKEN von Zernwitz & Wenglaus: Or, three fishes naiant in pale Argent finned Gules.

4. p.CXCI: HARTUNG DE CLUGX, ANGLICUS, miles: Sable, on a fess Argent three ducks Or.

5. p.XCVI: DER GRAFF (Count) VON ULTINGEN: Argent, a stag springing Or attired Gules.

6. p.CXCI: JOHANNES WATTERTHON ANGLICUS, miles: Per pale Argent, a chevron embowed gules and Argent, a fleur-de-lis Or.

7. p.CLXVI: WILHALM SCHENCK VON SYDAW auss Sachsen: Argent, a horshoe in bend with an arrow point issuing towards the dexter chief Or.

8. p.XC: Von dem hochgebornen Edlen HERZOGEN (Duke) VON ROTEN REÜSSEN: Per fess in chief Argent, three crosses Or and in base Sable, a demi-eagle with two heads Or.

9. p.CXLVIII: Von dem hochgebornen Fürsten/Herzog (Prince/Duke) VON OPPOLIENEC us dem Konigreich Polen: Argent, an eagle Or crowned and legged Gules.

10. p.CLXXI: Heinrich VON DER END & Condradt von der End: Or, a fox with a duck in his jaws Argent.

11. p.CX: Dominus ELIBORI Episcopus Agrinensis inn Rome, bears inn the second and third quarter: Argent, issuing from a boat Or a wolf's head and neck Sable. The same as is borne in their first and fourth quarters, page CLVIII: Scieber Graff zu STIEBORCZ VON PLONCZG UND WAYDEN inn syben burgen, and, reverse: Graff SCIEBORN VON SCIEBORN HERR AM WAG.

Plate VIII

12. p.CXCIII: Jannue de Saragusa, Argent, a boar salient Or.

Plate VIII

The *Ancien Armorial equestre de la Toison d'or et de l'Europe au 15e siècle* also contains a number of Or and Argent arms. We have reproduced some examples in colour (without blazoning) from this Armorial.

ÉCUS D'ALLEMAGNE (plate XLI)
1. Elkinge, Burgau (Berg, margrave de Burgau, appears also in the third quarter of the Royal Bavarian Majestätswappen, see Hupp, *Münchener Kalender*, 1906).

2. Drochzes Libman von TRUSCH.

3. Gayman Geumanner.

4. Dost von Dosse (plate XLIII).

5. Frisztorfer ... Friesdorf.

ÉCUS DE HOLLANDE (plate LI)
6. Hassendelf... Assendelft.

7. Mordrech... Moordrecht.

ÉCUS D'ARTOIS (plate XXXIX)
8. Mons. d'Avelnies... Avelny.

ÉCUS DE POLOGNE, (plate CVII)
9. Le s. de Capiense, de Kepinsky, plate CX.

10. Jehan Rasperolla.

A great number of countries, provinces, cities, towns and villages have gold and silver arms. We give only a few instances from different countries:

11. The arms of the village of BRIENZ, near Interlaken, Canton Bern, designed by Paul Boesch, see Hag, *Armorial de la Suisse*, fascicule 6, n. 224, p.23.

12. The arms of the City of COPENHAGEN date from 1250.

(See S.T. Achen, *Danmarks Kommunevaabner*, p.21. In this volume we find about a dozen examples of Argent and Or combinations adopted between 1300 and 1977).

13. The arms of LA CHAUX-DE-FONDS, canton de Neuchâtel, Switzerland, see Hag, *Armorial de la Suisse*, fascicule 6, n.181, p.13.

14. The arms of CIUDAD REAL in Spain were granted by King Alfonso the Wise (1221-1284), see Louda, *European Civic Coats of Arms*, p.120.

15. The arms of JYVÄSKYLÄ, a Finnish town; see *Avain Omaan Maahan Viikkosanomat*, 1964, p.125. There are more Or and Argent arms, most of them adopted in the 20th century. In *Suomen Kunnallisvaakunat*, 1970, the boat is red and not gold.

16. SCHAFFHAUSEN is the capital of the Swiss canton of the same name. See Louda, *European Civic Coats of Arms*, p.218.

17/18. PILSEN, the largest city in Bohemia, has Argent, two keys Or in the first quarter.

SALAMANCA, the famous Spanish University town, has in the sinister part: Argent, on a bridge Or a bull Sable under a tree Vert, see Louda, p.214.

19. CYPRUS in 1960 adopted Gold, a white dove volant with a green leaf in its beak. See Smith, *Zeichen der Menschen & Völker*, p.320, n.2.

20. The arms of NORD TROENDELAG in Norway were created in 1957 by the famous Norwegian State Archivist and Heraldist Halvard Trätteberg. See Cappelen, *Norske Communevapen*, p.183.

21. AUSCHWITZ (Oswiecim, a Polish town near the ill-famed Nazi extermination camp, has very fine arms: Azure, a double headed eagle Argent with a triple-towered castle Or on its chest. See Louda, *European Civic Coats of Arms*, p.196. These arms date from 1793.

22. The flag of the KURDS, ethnic minority, persecuted in Iraq, Iran and Turkey, is Tierced per fess Vert, Argent and Gules, a sun Or over all. See Smith, *Zeichen der Menschen & Völker*, p.320, n.2. In this volume we find many more examples of Or upon Argent as, for instance, the Kingdom of Tonga which bears in the first quarter Argent, three stars Or; and in the fourth quarter, Argent, three swords Or.

Plate IX Plate IX

L'Armorial Miltenberg is a very fine armorial from the end of the XVth century published by Dr Jean-Claude Loutsch, President of the International Heraldic Academy, in *Archives Héraldiques Suisses*, 1989/II, 1990/I & II and 1991/I. We show here nine examples:

1. p.106, Fo. 24r: Der kunig von der GROSSEN NORWARTT: Or, three swans Argent.

2. p.150, Fo. 26v: Priester JOHAN: Argent, a lion Or turned to sinister holding a cross Gules.

3. p.181 Fo. 28v: Der künig von jherusalem: Argent, a patriarchal cross Or issuant from a triple mount Or.

4. p.706, Fo. 57v: GRUNENBERG: Argent, two tertres Vert of three (peaks) bordered (en haut) Or one over the other.

5. p. 801 Fo. 62v: ECHTER: Azure, on a bend Argent three rings Or.

6. p.833, Fo. 64v: EINSIEDLER: Or, a hermit vested Argent holding a stick with his dexter hand Argent and in his sinister a stick of the same with a bunch of grapes Vert hanging on it.

7. p.937 Fo. 70v: ROCKENEHER: Tierced per bend Gules, Argent and Sable, on the Argent three garbs Or.

8. p.983 Fo. 70v: LOEWENSTEIN: Argent, a lion rampant Gules crowned Or upon a triple mountain Or.

9. p.1056 Fo. 77r: DIE BURGRAFFEN: Gules, a bend Argent, an escarbuncle fleur-de-lisé Or over all.

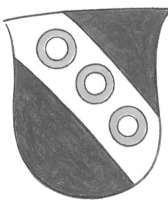

Plate X
Plate X

On this plate we bring some instances from a private Manuscript from the time of Queen Elizabeth (ca 1570) owned by Cecil R. Humphery-Smith, Principal of the Institute of Heraldic & Genealogical Studies in Canterbury (MS 5401).

1. p.4: AGREVOLL: Or, a lion rampant reguardant Argent.

2. p.10: ANNELSLEY: Per pale Or and Argent, a dog (mastiff or talbot) statant Gules.

3. p.28: EDWARDS OF EARTOR: Per bend sinister Argent and Sable, a lion rampant over all Or.

4. p.29: DANUCO: Per pale Argent and Or, a lion's head erased Gules.

5. p.36 HAYWARD OF GLOSTERSHIR: Argent, three barrulets Sable and over all three cotton hanks Or.

6. p.47 MOOR OF ASTORNBACH: Paly of six Or and Argent, a lion rampant Sable over all.

7. p.99: SATTON OF BARKSHIR: Or, a lion rampant Vert and a fess Argent over all.

8. p.137: THOMAS POWELL of Wittington in Shropshire: Quarterly Or and Argent, a lion rampant Gules over all.

More instances from another English Manuscript (ca 1563) also belonging to Cecil Humphery-Smith.

A TUDOR ARMORIAL
9. p.31: SIR FRANCIS JOBSON: Paly of six Argent and Azure, a chevron Ermine between three eagles displayed Or over all, granted to Sir Francis Jobson *ca* 1550.

10. p.41: HARLSTON: Argent, a quadrangular fret Or fimbriated Gules.

11. p.59: BARNEBE: Per pale nebuly Argent and Or, three boars' heads couped Sable, tusked Argent, langued Gules.

12. p.97: MR HORSHAM: Azure, three bends Argent each charged with three mullets Or.

Plate XI

13. p.103: MR DARRYLL: Azure, a lion rampant Or with a trefoil slipped Argent on the shoulder.

14. p.157: MR SVYNTLEGIER: Azure fretty Argent and a bordure indented Argent, a chief Or. (This may appear to be a rather marginal example, but a chief is an ordinary. Were it a fess or a saltire it would be more noticeable. Mr P. W. Stanford of Colne, Lancashire, cites a well evidenced example of a grant of arms by Christopher Barker, Garter King of Arms, in 1542: Argent, three bars Azure, a canton Or thereon a fess and in chief three mascles Sable. Such instances are not infrequent but often, like this one, represent the overlaying of a distinct coat, not of an ordinary in its own right. This example equates with impaled or quartered coats in which gold and silver may be juxta-positioned and unavoidable).

Plate XI

General Armory Two by Cecil R. Humphery-Smith, 1984, has more than thirty examples of Argent and Or combinations, mostly from the 14th to 17th centuries:

1. p.2: ADERONNE (Co. Surrey): Argent, a chevron Or.

2. p.41: COLBROKE: Argent, a lion rampant Gules debruised by a fess Or.

3. p.60: FAUCONER, (Hurst, Co. Kent): Quarterly Argent and Azure, a falcon Or over all.

4. p.67: FREEMAN: Or, a chevron between three fleurs-de-lis per pale Argent and Gules.

5. p.90: HUMEZ: Quarterly Or and Azure, a lion rampant Argent.

6. p.110: MAUNSELL: Argent, a tower Sable having a scaling ladder raised against it in bend sinister Or (See also Papworth p.364).

Plate XII

7. p.111: MEGGS (Darnam, Co. Cambridge): Or, a chevron Argent between three mascles Gules on a chief Sable a wolf courant Argent.

8. p.113: MONMOUTH: Or, three chevrons Gules over all a fess Argent. Sir John de Monemouth.

9. p.123: PEMBRIDGE: Argent, a chief Azure over all a bend engrailed Or. Sire Johan de Pembruge.

10. p.132: RINGWOOD: Argent, a chevron compony (counter-compony) Sable and Or between three moorcocks of the second.

11. p.140: SENNYLE: Argent, a bend between six crosses crosslet fitchy Or. Sir Simon de Sennyle.

12. p.150: SUTTON: Or, a lion rampant tail forked Vert over all on a fess Argent three torteaux Gules. James Sutton of Chester.

Plate XII

In *Papworth's Ordinary*, if time is taken to go carefully through the 1200 pages, well over 200 instances of Or and Argent will be found and even more colour upon colour. Here are a few examples:

1. p.62: Argent, a lion rampant Azure depressed by a bend Or: Faulconbridge and the same with a bendlet Or: SIR WALTER FAULCONBRIDGE, Essex, *tempore* Edward III (1312-77).

2. p.64: Argent, a lion rampant Gules over all a bend raguly Or: STEWART, Norfolk (before Henry VIII).

3. p.90: Per pale Gules and Or, a lion rampant Argent: AUGUSTINIAN PRIORY at KIRKBY BELLERS, Co. Leicester.

4. p.137: Argent, a lion rampant between four crescents in square Or, on a chief Azure three mullets of the field. RUSSELL, LONGRIDGE.

5. p.417: Argent, a chevron between three estoiles of eight points wavy Or: WISEMAN, Scotland.

6. p.622: Quarterly Or and Gules, a cross of lozenges Argent, in the dexter chief an eagle of the last: FODRINGEY. See Glover's *Ordinary*, Cotton MS; MS *Tiberius*, p.6; Harl. MS. 1392.

7. p.925: Per bend crenelly Argent and Gules, three boars' heads couped Or: PETERS, Co. Aberdeen.

8. p.968: Argent, three lozenges Or within a bordure Ermine: GALLOWAY.

9. p.15: Argent, two bars Gules, overall a cross in bend sinister Or: PRIORY at Sempringham, Co. Lincoln.

10. p.20: Argent, two bars Sable in the dexter chief a quatrefoil Or: SIRE JOHN DE TWYFORD (1322), Boroughbrige Roll.

11. p.196: Quarterly Gules and Or, a bend Argent: (Fitz-Nicoll) STEPHEN LANGTON, Archbishop of Canterbury (1207-1228).

12. p.455: Argent, a chevron Ermine between three lions' gambs erased Or, armed Gules: WHITWANGE, Harl. MS 1404, fo.120.

13. p.758: Or, a fess chequy Azure and Argent between two garbs in chief and in base a crescent of the second: STEWART, Till the Cap, Co. Banff, Scotland.

14. p.752: Argent, a fess Gules, overall two dolphins hauriant respecting each other Or, the space between the dolphins Ermine: BUCKLAND.

15. p.778: Argent, a fess Gules between three saltires Or: SEWALL DE BOVILL, Archbishop of York (1256-1258).

16. p.1044: Argent, a land tortoise Or, on a chief Azure a mullet of the second between two bezants: GOLDIE, Scotland.

17. p.1071: Argent, a saltire engrailed between four escallops Or: William Beveridge, Bishop of St Asaph (1704-1708).

18. p. 1100: Argent, a sun eclipsed issuing from the dexter chief, the beams Or: Welday, Wheelhurst, Randle Holme.

Plate XIII

Plate XIII

The *Codice Cremosano* is also a fine and monumental Italian heraldic record. This manuscript was composed in 1673 by Marco Cremosano. We have examined it three times in the Biblioteca del Senato in Milan. It contains well over 500 examples of arms with combinations of gold and silver. They are not blazoned but well designed and very clearly coloured. We have simply quoted the names of the families concerned and indicated the pages where examples can be checked. These speak for themselves.

1. Antiani, p.10.

2. Alegrini, p.10.

3. Assini, p.16 (canting arms: *asino* = ass).

4. Bonadies, p.28.

5. Bicinatti, p.30.

6. Bonaghi, p.40.

7. Corbello, p.63 (allusive arms: German Korb, Italian *corba* meaning basket; *corbello*, back-basket).

8. Fiocchi, p.121 (again canting arms, *fiocchi* meaning tassels).

9. Secco, p.167.

10. Guerra, p.139.

11. Pizzoni, p.237.

12. Petramala d'Arezzo, p.243.

Plate XIV   Plate XIV

Siebmacher's *Grosses und allgemeines Wappenbuch*, Facsimile Reprint of the twelve Supplements from 1753-1806.

There are over 4,000 coats of arms figured. More than 200 of them have Or and Argent one upon the other or side by side. This is about 5% and we may suppose that such a percentage applies more or less to the whole of Siebmacher's armorial collection which is, of course drawn, from all over Europe. (See Jäger-Sunstenau, *General Index*).

Horst Appuhn has published (1988) Siebmacher's *Armorial* of 1605 in colour. We show on Plate XIV, 23 our rendering of some of them quoting the Supplements (S) and Appuhn's coloured edition (1988) (A).

1. Baron (Freiherr) ERMANS: they are not blazoned but coloured S II, p.11.

2. Baron RUPA, A, p.28.

3. Baron RIEDHEIM, S, IIII, p.22 & A, p.30.

4. Baron ALTENSTEIN, S, III, p.3.

5. PENZ in Holstein & Mecklenburg, S, IIII, p.2.

6. von VOHENSTEIN, S, IIII, p.27 & A. p.116.

7. von FONTIN, S, XI, p.9

8. von MERSUCKHOFEN, A, p.90.

9. von ANNENBERG, A, p.43

10. Baron von ERNAU, A, p.46 & S, XII, p.20.

11. Fürsten (Princes) DIETRICHSTEIN, S, VI, p.l.

12. von BEDAW, A, p.62.

13. von HABERKORN, A, p.105..

14. von HABSPERG, A, p.110.

15. von GREFEN, A, p.153.

16. Die MONSIART ET ARINO, S. VIII, p.21.

17. von GÖRLITZ, A, p.156.

18. Die KUNOVIDT, A, p.179.

19. (the city of EYSTATT (Eichstätt), A, p.220.

20. (the town of) SULTZBACH, A, p.220.

21. (the town of) LICHENAW, A, p.221.

22. (the town of) ROSSPACH, A, p.223.

23. (the town of) TUTTLINGEN, A, p.226.

(And 12 more towns, Appuhn)

Plate XV

The VICOMTE DE MAGNY in the *Dictionnaire Héraldique* preceding his *Armorial Général des Familles nobles d'Europe* (which, however, contains mostly French arms and only a few from other countries) notes under the heading ENQUERRE, p. CVIII: "on ne doit jamais sur un écu, poser métal sur métal, ni couleur sur couleur. Les cas exceptionnels son très rares et se disent à ENQUERRE, parce qu'il doit y avoir un motif a cette dérogation aux règles absolues du blason". He provides some kind of reason as to why the arms of Godefroy de Bouillon were Argent upon Or: They were adopted in 1099, before heraldry existed and the reasons were given later. I would say that in 1099 no one was fussy but found it very suitable. I would find it worthwhile to ask why there are very many families who include the Cross of Jerusalem in their armorial bearings. Often their qualification may be rather far-fetched unless they can prove that they really descended from a King of Jerusalem.

A good number of de Magny's French arms are examples of colour on colour. Whether he calls it "cousu" or not makes no difference. This sounds rather like some kind of subterfuge or excuse. Examples: p.2, n.10: Abric de Fenouillet: "d'azur, au chevron cousu de gueules . . . " and p.28, n.158:

Les comtes de Valleton: "d'azur, à une fasce cousu de gueules).* He has, however, also about 40 examples of metal upon metal of which on this plate we give the following instances:

1. p.92, n.584: DE COSNE: d'azur, au chevron d'argent, une fasce d'or brochant.

2. p.154, n. 1258: D'YONNE: de gueules, un pal d'argent, chaussé d'or.

3. p.163, n.1320: DE MONTFORT: d'argent, à la croix de gueules gringolée d'or.

4. p.164, n.1323: DE LAVISEZ: d'or, à une croix haussée d'argent soutenue d'un croissant du même, et adextrée en chef d'une étoile d'or (armes à enquerre) – (But he does not enquire!)

5. p.189, RABIN DE LIGNAC, Poitou: d'argent à 4 burelles d'azur, et 3 chevrons d'or brochant sur le tout.

6. p.191: BAUDRY DE SEMILLY, Normandy: d'argent, au chevron d'or, accompagné en chef de deux croix de Malte d'or, et en pointe d'un trèfle d'argent.

7. p.194: BERTRAND DE MARIMONT, Lorraine: écartelé en sautoir d'or et d'argent, à la croix patée et alésée de sable brochant.

8. p.195: BEUGNY D'HAGERNE, Artois: d'argent, à l'aigle éployée de sable, au pairle d'or brochant sur le tout.

9. p.201: BROSSARD DE CORBIGNY, Beauce: tiercé en barre d'argent, d'hermine et d'or. I wonder why Ermine is not considered equally as indistinguishable upon gold as Argent is.

* We read in the *Annuaire Général Héraldique universel*: "cousu se dit des piéces de métal sur métal ou couleur sur couleur; ce qui est contraire aux règles du blason. Pour bien valoir, les figures doivent trancher sur un fond jaune ou blanc (or ou argent) et réciproquement. Mais on peut se dispenser de l'emploi du mot 'cousu' parce que cela se voit bien quand les règles ont été violées, sans qu'il soit nécessaire de le proclamer".

Plate XV

10. p.210: FOLLIOT DE CRENNEVILLE, Normandy: d'argent à la croix de Saint-André de gueules, à l'aigle d'or à deux têtes, le vol éployé, brochant sur le tout.

11. p.220: FOURNES DE LA BROSSE, Lyonnais, Languedoc et Dauphiné: d'argent à 3 fasces d'azure; et sur le tout, un griffon ailé d'or, onglé, langué et couronné d'azur.

12. p.223: GARNIER DU FOUGERAY, Brittany: parti d'or et d'azur; l'or chargé en pointe d'une coquille d'azur; l'azur chargé en chef d'une coquille d'or; à l'épée d'argent garni d'or, posée en bande, la pointe en haut, brochant.

13. p.225: DE GENTILS DE LANGALERIE, Limousin, Saintogne and Switzerland: d'azur, au chevron d'or, accompagné de 3 roues de Sainte Catherine du même; à l'épée nue d'argent, posée en pal, la pointe en haut, brochant sur le tout.

14. p.225: GIGOU DE LA CROIX, Poitou: d'argent au chevron de gueules, accompagné de 3 cigognes d'or, 2 en chef et une en pointe.

15. p.233: D'HESPEL, Artois: écartelé; aux premier et 4e, d'or à 3 ancolies d'azur, 2 et 1; aux 2e et 3e, d'argent au chevron parti d'or et d'azur.

16. p.237: DE LAGRENÉE, Picardy: de gueules au chevron d'or, accolé et enlacé d'un autre chevron renversé d'argent, mouvant du chef.

17. p.259: DOULCET DE PONTÉCOULANT, Normandy: d'argent à la croix de sable fleurdelisée d'or.

18. p.241: LE LIEUR DE VILLE-SUR-ARCE, Normandy Soissonais, Champagn and Ile-de-France: d'or à la croix endentée d'argent et de gueules, cantonnée de 4 têtes de léopard d'azur, lampassées de gueules.

19. p.270: LE MARQUIS DE SINNIBALDI, Tuscany: d'hermine à la bande d'or (armes à enquerre). Here de Magny seems to agree with me, while above (9), he does not say that one should enquire.

20. p.272 TEXTOR DE RAVIZI, Forez: d'argent, à l'épée d'or, pointe en haut, accompagnée de 3 étoiles de sable, 2 et 1.

Plate XVI
DENMARK

Plate XVI

To find Danish examples of Or and Argent arms we make use of Professor Herman Storck's *Nyt Dansk Adels Lexikon* and of Sven Tito Achen's *Danske Adelsvåbener*. Achen has blazoned Storck's rich collection of over 1,700 coats of arms of Danish noble families from the Middle Ages until the XIXth century. For about 500 of them Achen could not give the tinctures. Among those he was able to blazon we find more than sixty Or and Argent. We give here fifteen of them indicating the pages where they can be verified in Achen's book using the original designs of Storck, and two of the many to be found in Rolland's *Rietstap*.

1. p.387: VON PODEWILS (Uradel of Pomerania): Per fess Argent and chequy Or and Azure, a demi stag issuing from the base.

2. p.405: SCHUMACHER (Ambassador Peter Chr. Schumacher ennobled 1782): Within a bordure Or a bar Or in chief Argent and Gules divided by a pallet Or, in base Vert, three hearts Gules.

3. p.39: VON PULTZ (1686): Argent, a lion rampant Or holding a ball Sable. Also in Rolland's *Rietstap*, Vol.V, Plate CVII.

4. p.399: PUDER (Uradel from Jutland, 1367): Quarterly Gules and Argent, a fess Or over all.

5. p.411: GÅS i FYN (Uradel): Or, on a fess Gules three eggs Argent, in chief three geese heads and necks Argent.

6. p.400: AMBRING (Tord Ambring, Knight in Jutland 1312): Gules, two pales Argent a fess Or over all.

7. p.400: HOHENDORFF (Uradel from Brandenburg): Argent, two pales Gules and Or a fess Azure over all.

8. p.108: LUND (Uradel from South Jutland): Argent, an eagle Sable, a star Or instead of the head.

9. p.366: MUNTHE AF MORGENSTIERNE (Bredo von Munthe til Baekkeskov was ennobled in 1755. The famous Swedish physician and author Axel Munthe was a member of this family): Per fess Argent and Gules, in chief a mullet of eight points Or above two wooden branches in saltire proper in base three plates Argent.

Plate XVII

10. p.410: BELDENAK (ennobled 1511): Or, a fess wavy Azure with an increscent Argent over all.

11. p.475: DE THYGESEN (Jesper and Lars Thygesen were ennobled 1776): Argent, two wheat ears issuant from a hill Vert between them a mullet of eight points and a chevron over all Or. (See also in Rolland's plates from *Rietstap*, Vol.VI, Plate XXVIII).

12. p.299: SADERSEN: Per saltire Or and Gules, a fleur-de-lis Argent over all. (See Rolland's *Rietstap*, Vol. V, Plate CCXX).

13. p.299: WALTER (ennobled 1649): Per pale Argent and Azure, in the sinister a dented wheel Or.

14. STAVENVOET (Hans Stavenvoet received his patent of nobility in 1476): Per pale Argent and Azure, a crowned lion statant Or over all with a heart Gules in his mouth.

15. NAVESEN: Argent, a mullet of six points between two demi fleurs-de-lis per bend and bend sinister Or. (Rolland's *Rietstap*, Vol.IV, Plate CCLXXIII).

Plate XVII
FRANCE

In the *Annuaire Général Héraldique Universel* of 1901 we find over forty examples of Or and Argent arms. Half of them are illustrated and half are clearly blasoned:

1. p.246: D'ASSCHE, Marquis: Or, five escallops in cross Argent.

2. p.393: DE BRESSON, Comte: Argent, an arrow in pale Gules surmounted by a saltire couped Or, between in fess two crescent's horns uppermost in chief and base four mullets all Gules.

3. p.574: D'EON DE BEAUMONT, Marquis in Brittany: Per pale Argent and Or, a lion rampant counterchanged armed and crowned Gules.

4. p.651: GIROD DE L'AIN, Baron: Tierced in bend Or, Argent and Sable, a chevron Argent over all.

5. pp.592 and 593: DE FAURE et du Faure de Saint-Martial: Azure, a bend Argent enfiled with three coronets Or.

Plate XVIII

6. p.371: BOULIN DE BEYSSERAT: Or, three trefoils slipped Argent (2 & 1).

7. p.1084: DES ROYS, Vicomte: Argent, a bend Gules between three mullets, two in chief and one in base Or.

8. p.661: GOURY DE ROSLAN, Baron: Or, three bends Argent.

9. p.592: FAULTE DE VANTEAUX, Comte: Argent, a tree erased Vert and a lion passant guardant Or over all.

10. p.732: DE KERTANGUY, Vicomte: Argent, a boar's head erased Sable, in chief a ducal coronet Or.

11. p.738: DE LABBÉ DE CHAMPGRAND, Comte: Argent, three bars Gules, a lion rampant and crowned Or over all.

12. p.832: LE GOUZ DE SAINT-SEINE, Marquis, from Brittany, 1442 established in Burgundy: Gules, a cross Argent indented Or cantoned by four spearheads Argent.

13. p.1130: DE TAPPIE DE VINSAC, Baron: Argent, a lion rampant Or and in base a crescent also Or, on a chief Azure three mullets of six points Argent.

14. p.1137: DE TERZY, Marquis: Argent, seven lozenges conjoined in bend double cotised all Or.

May we add two fine examples from Guérin de la Grasserie's *Armorial de Bretagne*:

Jean Conen

Seigneur de Perpéan et du Pontiguet 1669

Eon Conen, 1400

Vol.I, p.131, n.51

Julien de la Villette 1669

Bertand de la Villette 1486

Vol.I, p.131, n.51

Plate XVIII
IRELAND

In Irish heraldry Or/Argent combinations are rather frequent. In the *Atlas and Cyclopedia of Ireland* which illustrates coats of arms of leading lrish families (Dublin, 1904) some thirty-six of 480 arms are gold and silver, i.e. well over 7%, while Vert/Or are about 3%, colour on colour about 5%, Gules/Argent about 26%. The arms are not blazoned but clearly coloured.

1. CHRISTY: *Atlas*, Plate 15, n.177, and *Kennedy's Book of Arms*, p.5.

2. LEBAS: *Kennedy,* p.13

3. HOW: *Kennedy,* p.147.

4. MCGILL: *Atlas*, Plate 7, n.7.

5. EGAN: *Atlas*, Plate 16, n.66.

6. O'ROURKE: *Atlas*, Plate 4, n.82.

7. FERGUSON: *Atlas*, Plate 26, n.241.

8. BREEN: *Atlas*, Plate 26, n 283.

9. LOGAN: *Atlas*, Plate 16, n.294.

10. FAULKNER: *Atlas*, Plate 7, n.307.

11. FANNING: *Atlas*, Plate 34, n.336, and *Heraldic Scroll of Ireland.*

12. PURCELL: *Atlas*, Plate 18, n.339.

13. DEVINE: *Atlas*, Plate 37, n.371.

14. GRIFFIN: *Atlas*, Plate 5, n.373.

15. ENGLISH: *Heraldic Scroll of Ireland.*

16. GILROY: *Atlas*, Plate 8, n.56.

(The numbering in the *Atlas* is absolutely extraordinary and is not consecutive).

Plate XIX
POLAND

For Polish instances, we have consulted two sources: *Polskiej Akademii* Nauk: *Herby rycerstwa polskiego* & Ostrowski, Juliusz Hr: *Ksiega Herbowna Rodóv Polskich.*

1. The BIAŁEGA family bears: Or, a bend wavy 17 humetty bendwise Argent. (See Ostrowski, n.143).

2. The Counts SKRZYNSKI bear: Per fess Purpure, a demi lion Sable issuant from a wall embattled and masoned Argent with three of the stones Or. (See Ostrowski, n. 3440).

The Skrzynskis belong to the armorial clan Zaremba with a group of twenty-one families using the same arms. (See *Polskiej Akademii*: Zaremba).

3. The OSICIMSKI family bears: Argent, a horse-shoe with a crosslet on the top and one below all Or. (See Ostrowski, n. 2416).

4. The GRABIE family bears: Or, a rake with seven teeth Argent. (See Ostrowski, nn. 883, 884 & 885).

5. The Princes SIESICKI bear: Or, a hippocentaur shooting with a crossbow against his tail ending in a serpent's head Argent. (See Ostrowski, n. 3395. The Polish blazoning is abundant in words and often very simply descriptive).

6. The HOLOWIŃSKI family bears: Argent, issuant from two hills Vert a cross with a crescent traversing the stem Or. (See Ostrowski, n. 1046).

7. The BROCHWICZ family bears: Or, a stag issuant from a crescent reversed over a star of six points all Argent. (See Ostrowski, n. 280).

8. The Counts OSTROWSKI bear: Or, a crowned lady Argent sitting on a bear passant Sable. (See Ostrowski, n. 2453, and *Polskiej Akademii*. The Ostrowskis belong to the Rawicz armorial clan).

9. The GROTY family bear: Or, three tops of spears Argent. (See Ostrowski, n. 921).

Plate XIX

10. The MONCZ family bear: Argent, an arrow issuing from a letter M and slipping through an annulet Or. (See Ostrowski, n. 2126).

11. The REMBOWSKI family bear: Argent, three stars of six points Or over three wedge-shaped mountain peaks Vert. (See Ostrowski, n. 3074).

12. The CHORYNSKI family bear: Or, two buffalo horns the dexter Sable with three lobster claws Argent, the sinister Argent with three lobster claws Sable. (See Ostrowski, n. 383).

This is a selection of Polish Or/Argent arms. Some of them are shared by many families with different names as, for instance, the Korzbok group: Argent, three fishes naiant towards the sininster Or. These arms are borne by ten families. The Rawicz clan, with the Counts Ostrowski, has 120 families using the same arms, and as already noted, the Zaremba clan comprises twenty-one families with different names (see *Polskiej Akademii* Nauk).

Plate XX
PORTUGAL

The *Anuário da Nobreza de Portugal* is of no help. It does not blason the arms; for example, the arms of the Marquês de Alegrete: Quarterly 1 & 4, Teles de Menezes, 2 & 3, Silva.

The Gold and Silver arms illustrated on this plate are taken from the *Armorial Lusitano* by Doutor Martins Zúquete (AL) and from the *Livro do Armeiro-Mor* by João Du Cros (AM).

1 QUEIMADO (medieval): Or, two wolves passant in pale Gules in chief St Anthony's cross (Tau cross) Argent (AL p. 455).

2. NETO (Petro Neto is mentioned as a witness in a document of 1168): Per pale Gules and Azure, a lion Or over all, on a border Or four fleurs-de-lis Argent between four fig leaves Vert (AL p. 392).

Plate XX

3. LACUEVA: Argent, on a pile issuant from the base Or, between two palets Gules a dragon Vert, all within a bordure Gules charged with eight saltires Or (AL p. 289).

4. REGO (time of Kings Sancho II, 1223-45, and Alfonso III 1238-79: Vert, on a bend wavy Argent three escallops Or (AL p.466 & AM pp. 135 & 277).

5. LORONHA; Per pale Argent and Vert, on the dexter a demi-fleur-de-lis Or united per pale with a demi-rose Gules . . . etc (AL p. 315).

6. VALEJO (XVIth century): Or, five bendlets Azure within a bordure Ermine with a saltire Or in chief. This is an instance of many arms not blazoned Or and Argent although appearing so (AL p. 538).

7. GODIZ: Chequy Or and Argent (AM pp. 122 & 249).

8. DE BENEVIDES (from the time of Alfonso VII): Argent, a lion bendy Or and Gules (AL pp. 94/95).

9. CARDUCHO: Barry of eight Argent and Azure, over all a bend Or (AL p. 138).

10. IMPERIAL (Frederico Imperial gave proof of noble descent in 1529): Argent, on a broad pale Or an eagle displayed Sable crowned Or (AL p. 279).

11. COIMBRA (Vicente Diaz de Coimbra was chief justice in 1249): Or, a thistle Vert in dexter chief point a mullet Argent, all within an orle of knotted cord Argent (AL pp. 169/170).

12. VISME: Argent, a chevron Gules between two mullets in chief and a crescent in base Or (AL p. 561).

13. LEY: Or, six cotices in bend Argent (AM pp. 134 & 276).

14. ROCHA: Argent, on a saltire Gules between four escallops an escallop all Or (AM pp. 135 & 278).

15. ANTAN: Vert, on a bend Argent two lions passant Or (AM pp. 129 & 264).

16. PEDROSA: Or, five stones Argent, the one in the centre charged with an eagle Sable (AM p. 105).

AM p. 105
Pedrosa: Or five stones Argent, the one in the centre charged with an eagle Sable

Plate XXI

Plate XXI

Plate XXI
RUSSIA

In Russia until the early XVIIIth century and even later the significance of colours and their almost mystical interpretation was strongly influenced by the Byzantine tradition. Gold and Silver (yellow and white) have almost supernatural meaning and therefore the "bimetallism" (the Or and Argent combination) in early Russian heraldry was hardly considered as wrong, but rather with awe, as an expression of sublimity and solemnity.

We are grateful to Mikhail Yurievich Medvedev from St Petersburg for the examples illustrated on this plate. His heraldic design is so good that we prefer to reproduce these Russian examples painted by himself with heartfelt thanks for his permission.

1. The arms of the POYARKOV family: Azure, an escutcheon Or charged with an eagle Argent between in chief a coronet Or and in base on a mount Vert a helmet Proper.

2. The armorial achievement of the PRINCES AMILAKHVARI is a Georgian instance. Even the white mantling is scattered with golden flowers. In a letter dated 21st September 1845 Prince Teimouraz of Georgia wrote to Count I.O. Simonich that the white mantle means purity of heart and the golden flowers are a symbol of princely grandeur (see *The Heraldic Researcher* St Petersburg, June 1913, pp.105-106). The shield in the centre is: Or, an angel (Gabriel) vested Gules, the wings Argent.

3. The BENOIS family (of French origin) ennobled in Russia bear: Azure, a column Argent issuing from the base charged with a golden cross between two fleurs-de-lis Or, a chief Ermine.

4. The arms of the PACHOLOWIECKI family are partly a variation of the arms of the Polish Jelita (Zamoyski) clan: Per pale Gules and Argent, a demi-eagle issuant from the dexter palar line Argent armed and crowned Or and two spears in saltire and one reversed per pale on the sinister all Or.

5. Of the same inspiration with different "bimetallism" are the arms of the VORONTSOV-VELYAMINOV family: Per pale Or and Gules, a demi-eagle Argent crowned Or on the dexter, and three lances two in saltire and one in pale Argent points downwards Or and their pomells also Gold, on the sinister.

6. The arms of the Princes DASHKOV are: Quarterly, 1 & 4, Azure, an angel (St Michael) vested Argent, armed Or; 2 & 3, Gules on a mount Vert a gun Sable with a bird of paradise on top of it Proper. While this is a curiosity, we are only interested in the escutcheon of pretence Argent, a cross botonny issuant from a figured crescent reversed over a star of six points all Or (called "koribut"). The Dashkovs are descended from Prince Rurik, the founder of the Russian State.

7. The arms of the PUSHCHIN family are quartered: 1 and 4, Azure, between two spades in saltire argent in chief a coronet Or; 2 & 3, Or, an eagle Argent with the regalia in its claws. Originally this eagle was Sable but in the late XVIIIth century shortly before the matriculation the tincture of the eagle was changed and the regalia appeared in his claws to make it more magnificent and more regal!

8. The arms of the BYCHKOV-ROSTOVSKI family (also descended from Rurik) are: Quarterly, Azure, Or, Purpure and Gules, over all a star of six points Argent above a figured crescent of the same, in base Or two sturgeons in saltire Argent.

The Or and Argent combinations were valued as the most solemn combinations. Already in the pre-heraldic time they appear in the state emblems of Russia. The Great Banner of the Tzars in the XVIIIth century was white with a golden double-headed eagle. Or and Argent were the patriotic colours.

Plate XXII
SPAIN

In Spanish heraldry, arms with Or and Argent are frequent even if we do not count the over-numerous bordures and disregard the evasive term "proper" (de su color).

It is not our task to present all the existing "exceptions" or to comb the entire literature in order to find yet more and more of them. On this plate we show just eight beautiful Spanish examples:

1. Here we have the arms of the DAS SEIXAS (XIIIth century): Gold, five pigeons volant Argent. (See *Pardo de Guavara*, p.99).

Plate XXII

2. In the armorial *Heráldica del Toso d'Or de Barcelona* from 1519 we find the arms of Don Alvaro de ZUÑIGA, Duque de Bejar, Marqués de Gibraleon, Conde de Vanares: Argent, a bend Sable, over all a chain Or in the form of an orle. (See *de Riquer*, Vol.II, p.728, fig.319).

3 The house of FERNANDEZ DE VALDERNA bears: Argent, above waves Azure and Argent a dolphin hauriant Or. (See de Cadenas, *Heráldica Patronímica*, p.62).

4. The LOPEZ (of Toledo, Ciudad Real, Guadalajara and Albacete) bear: Argent, two wolves Sable in a bordure Or charged with eight saltires [aspas] Azure. (Or, a border Argent, and vice versa, is very frequent in Spain). We give this instance as representative of many and we do NOT count them as giving the number of Or/Argent examples in quoted armorials.

5. The GONZALEZ DE RUEDA bear: Argent, a palace Or with a bordure compony Gules and Or. (See de Cadenas, p.114).

6. The SAN MARTIN bear: Argent, three bars compony countercompony Argent and Or. (See de Cadenas, p.256).

7. De RIQUER, Vol. II p.384, shows from the *Armorial of Salamanca XVIth century* fol.25, eleven arms blazoned: Argent, a pale Azure two rectangular flaunches overall Or each charged with a fig leaf of the second, appearing in as many as eleven coats of arms.

8. The MERLES DE MALLA bear canting arms: Wavy Argent and Sable, on a bend Or three blackbirds [merles] Sable. Note that the Spanish wavy is very particularly stylish leaving most of the bend on Argent. (see de Riquer Vol. II, p.406, n.9).

9. The MARTIN DE PEREDA bear: Argent, a church bell Or. (See de Cadenas, p.162).

10. The RODRIGUEZ DE ARELLANO bear: Argent, three lions' heads erased Or, langued Gules and dripping blood. (See de Cadenas, p.229).

11. Don José MUSLERA y Gonzalez de Burgos bears: Argent, a tree Vert surmounted in base by a wolf Sable and a lion passant Or in front of it. (See Instituto Salazar, *Blasonario*, p.108).

12. The SAN SALVADOR family bear: Or, five mullets in cross Argent. (See de Cadenas, p.259).

Don Vicente de Cadenas y Vicent de Castanaga y Nogues is the King of Arms of Spain, a Hidalgo of medieval extraction belonging to a family of counts. He bears in the second quarter of his arms Or, a bell Argent. In his *Heráldica Patronímica Española* he blazons over eight examples of Argent and Or arms for members of the Spanish nobility.

Don Francisco Piferrer in *Nobiliario de los Reinos y Señoríos de España* specifíes more than 140 Or with Argent arms. Perusing more armorials one would find more and more.

García de TUDELA: en plata dos cirios de oro con llamas de gules.

(See de Cadenas *Heráldica Patronímica* p.85)

Plate XXIII
SWEDEN

Plate XXIII

Many instances of Or and Argent are to be found in the Swedish *Adels Kalender*, (1947) over twenty (AK), and eighty-five in Jan Raneke's *Svensk Adels Heraldik* (R). Neither give any blazoning. The tinctures are clearly shown by hatching marks. We present here seven examples from AK and eight from R.

1. DE GEER AF FINSPÅNG and de Geer af Leufsta, Friherrer (Barons) known since 1300 (AK pp. 150-164).

2. GYLLENSPETZ, ennobled 1660 (AK p.307).

3. HAARD af Torestoop, known since 1490 (AK p. 385).

4. RUDEBECK, ennobled 1675 (AK p.690).

5. VON SALTZA known in Meissen since 1500, came to Sweden from Estonia, created Swedish Barons (Friherrer) 1755 and the "primo-genitus" became a count (Grev) in 1843. (AK p.697).

6. SILFWERBRAND, ennobled 1650. These are very typical Swedish canting arms, Silfwerbrand meaning argent – flaming torch (AK p. 165).

7. VON UNGERN-STERNBERG, Uradel (= nobility documented before 1400) from Livonia known since 1252, Barons of the Empire in Germany, recognised in Sweden in 1653 (AK p. 000).

8. KATARINA MÅNSDOTTER, ennobled 1568. Again canting arms, the name meaning moon's daughter. (R p. 82).

9. FREITAG, Uradel. (R p. 198).

10. ILLE, from Finland, recognised in Sweden 1625. (R p.213).

11. HIRSCHENSTIERNA, ennobled 1661 again canting arms, the name meaning stag's forehead (R p. 218).

12. STIERNSKÖLD, Uradel from Uppland, again: stars shield. (R p. 280).

13. SCOTT, Uradel from Scotland. (R p. 291).

14. STRAELBORN, recognised in Sweden in 1628. (R p. 298).

Plate XXIV

15. VON STACKELBERG, Uradel from Livonia, known since 1306, introduced in Sweden 1763 (Counts of the Holy Roman Empire) (R p. 331).

In Raneke's *Svensk Adels Heraldik*, over 3,400 arms (those found more than once counted as one) we have 2.5% Or and Argent combinations and over 7% colour upon colour.

Plate XXIV

On this last plate we show a number of particular Or and Argent arms:

1. The Barons (Freiherren) von OMPTEDA, Frisian Uradel (1317) [Uradel = nobility documented before 1400] bear: Argent, a double headed eagle Or. (See Hupp, *Münchener Kalender*, 1924).

2. The Princes (Fürsten) von REUSS. (See Hupp, *Münchener Kalender*, 1915). The Emperor Ferdinand I on 6th December 1561 added to the original arms of Reuss the second and third quarterings: Argent, a crane Or for the lordship of Kranichfeld – Hupp would have preferred Gules upon Or, but in spite of his pronounced adherence to the metal-colour rule he had to include eighteen examples of Or and Argent combinations among the arms in his *Münchener Kalenders.*

3. Friedrich von SCHILLER. When the famous German classic poet was elevated to the nobility of the Empire on 7th September 1802 he was given: Or, a unicorn Argent upon Azure, a bar Or. (see Gutmann Heft 14, year 1968).

4. Hans KRAMER was granted arms in Augsburg on 9th May 1574: Argent, a lion Or with a hood Sable round his head and neck. (Seyler, *Geschichte der Heraldik*, p.468). This design is made after a sketch by Michael Schroeder, Frankfurt a.m.

5. Sir John DE LA POLE, Duke of Suffolk (1442-92), had in the second and third quarters: Argent, a chief Gules with a lion rampant Or over all. (St John Hope, *Stall Plates of the Knights of the Garter* at St George's Chapel, Windsor, Plate LXXIX (date of the plate, *circa* 1472).

6. STEWART ERLE of Arrane has in the 8th and 14th quarters: Or, three cinquefoils Argent (Lyndsay of the Mount. *Facsimile of an Ancient Heraldic Manuscript* from 1542).

7. von ALTMANNSHAUSEN: Or, on a mountain Sable a shovel Argent pierced by a scythe blade of the same. (See: *Wappen und Ahnentafeln des Reichsgrafen Ferdinand Wilczek*, p.82, plate 13, n.200) The pedigree of Count Wilczek, who is the maternal grandfather of the reigning Prince of Liechtenstein, contains over thirty examples of arms with Or and Argent together. Many of these are repeated as many as ten times, so there is no mistake.

8. The King of CYPRUS is attributed: Or, a man's head in profile Sable hooded Argent. (See Humphery-Smith, *Anglo-Norman Armory. Two*, p.471. This ordinary of XIIIth century armorials contains more than a dozen Or and Argent coats and it is irrelevant whether all these arms were actually in use or only imaginary, what matters is that at that time no one seemed to mind).

9. The same is to be said of the arms of the Emperor of TREBIZOND in Grünenberg's *Wappenbuch*: Argent, a cockatrice Or. (see Ströhl: *Atlas*, plate XXX, n.2, quoting Grünenberg's beautiful *Armorial* (1462-83) which contains about seventy Or and Argent arms out of 2,133, that is, about 3.3%).

10. Nicolas DE LA SOUALLAYE, seigneur de Cavaro, 1669, bears: Argent, a stag's head caboshed Gules, its mouth pierced by an arrow Or. Olivier de la Souallaye lived in the fourteenth century. (See Guerin de la Grasserie, *Armorial de Bretagne*, Plate 121, n.71. This armorial contains nineteen examples of Or and Argent and about fifty of colour with colour called *cousu*, which, of course, does not change anything).

11. The armorial bearings of Raymond ANDREWS of Donnington Hayes, Berkshire, designed by Cecil Humphery-Smith and granted by the Garter King of Arms, Sir Colin Cole, and Clarenceux King of Arms, Sir Anthony Wagner, by Letters Patent dated as recently as 25th June 1986 do not avoid placing Argent upon Or and colour on colour.

12. BASEL. During the 101st General Assembly of the Société Suisse d'Héraldique, 13th/14th June 1992, in Basle, we visited the Council Hall of the Cantonal Government built in the early XVIth century. To my surprise I noticed on the carved

ceiling five shields Argent with the "Baselstab" (crozier) depicted in gold. The arms of the Bishop of Basle are Argent, a crozier Gules, and in the arms of the City of Basle the crozier is Sable. (Here I felt very strongly the need to make enquiries and I found out that in 1511 Pope Julius II (Giuliano della Rovere, 1503-1513) offered the City of Basle a banner and granted them the privilege that the crozier (*vulgo* Baselstab) formerly Sable be changed to Or: "in militarem colorem aureum libere et licite commutare valeant". They did so for a short time and when Œcolampadius, less than two decades later, introduced the Reformation they went back to the traditional Sable, but in the Council Hall the crozier remained preciously gilded until today.

The great number of regional civic armorials would yield many more instances of metal on metal.

13. HEIM: Argent, on a "Dreiberg" (triple mount) Vert a lion rampant Or holding a horseshoe Azure surmounted by a mullet of the third. These arms were painted on stained glass for Joh. Heimb in 1640. Joh. Heimb is the author's direct ancestor, n. 1024 on the pedigree, who died 15th February 1659. This explains why I have been looking for other instances of Or and Argent arms for very many years, and this book shows part of the harvest of my endeavours. (These arms are still publicly exposed in Boningen, Solothurn, Switzerland, two miles from where Johannes Heimb lived and had his house and land).

BIBLIOGRAPHY

The heraldic literature in the many European languages is so great that it would not be possible to survey it all; so we are bound to restrict ourselves to a modest selection.

ACHEN, Sven Tito, *Danske adelsvåbener en heraldisk nøgle*, Copenhagen, 1973. (Over 60 Or/Argent).

Danmarks kommunevaabner betw. 1250 1977, Copenhagen, 1967 & 1982. (Over 10 Or/Argent).

ADAM-EVEN, Paul, "L'Armorial du Héraut Gelre" in *Archives Héraldiques Suisses*, 1961-1968.

Annuaire Général Héraldique Universel de la Noblesse, Paris, 1901.

APPUHN, Horst, *Joh. Siebmachers Wappenbuch von 1605* (in colour) (110 Or/Argent).

Armorial Lusitano, Lisbon,1961.

BADO AUREO, Johannes de, *Tractatus de armis*, completed before 1394, edited by Sir Edward Bysshe, London, 1654.

BARTELEMY, Vincent, *Le Blason des Armoiries*, 1581.

BATY, Thomas, *Vital Heraldry*, Edinburgh,1962.

BERGMANS, Paul, *Armorial de Flandre du XVIe siècle*, Ghent,1919. (15 Or/Argent).

BISSAEUS, Edoardus (Sir Edward Bysshe), *Nicolai Uptoni de Studio Militari, Joh. de Bado Aureo: Tractatus de Armis, Henrici Spelmanni: Aspilogia*. London, 1654.

B(LUNT), E., *The Elements of Armories*, London,1610.

BERN, *Burgergemeinde*, illustrated by Paul Boesch, Bern, 1932. (Over 50 Or/Argent).

BOHET, P. et Willems, A., *Armorial Belge*, Bruxelles, 1961. (50 Or/Argent).

BOUTELL, Rev. Charles, *The Manual of Heraldry*, 1863; revised edition by J. P. Brooke-Little, London,1978.

BRAULT, Gerard, *Early Blazon: Heraldic Terminology in the XIIth & XIIIth centuries*, Oxford, 1972.

BURKE, Sir Bernard, *The General Armory of England, Scotland, Ireland & Wales*, comprising *A Registry of Armorial bearings from the earliest to the present time*, London,1880.

CADENAS Y VICENT, Vicente de, *Heráldica Patronímica Española*, Madrid, 1976. (Over 100 Or/Argent).

CAPPELEN, Hans & JOHANNESSEN, Knut, *Norske Kommunevåpen*, Oslo, 1987.

CASCANTE, Ignacio Vicente, *Heráldica General y Fuentes de las Armas de España*, Barcelona, 1956.

CHESSHYRE, Hubert & WOODCOCK, Thomas, *The Dictionary of British Arms, Medieval Ordinary*, Vol. I of four announced London, 1992. (32 Or/Argent).

CLARK, Hugh, *Introduction to Heraldry*, London, 1825, eighteenth ed. 1974. (Some Or/Argent).

CREMOSANO, Marco, MS *Codice Cremosano composto* 1673 kept in Archivio del Senato Milano. (over 500 Or/Argent examples).

CURTIN, J. C. and others, *Atlas and Cyclopedia of Ireland*, Dublin and New York, 1904. (Or/Argent 5%). Roll of Irish Heraldry, 1901.

DEAN, Dr. Ruth J., *An Early Treatise on Heraldry in Anglo-Norman*, Hayward, California, 1967.

DOUËT D'ARCQ, M. L., *Un traité de blason du XVe siècle in Revue Archéologique, cinquième et sixième livraison*.

DU CROS, João, *Livro do Armeiro-Mor*, Lisbon, 1956.

DUBUISSON, P. P., *Armorial alphabétique des principales maisons et familles du Royaume*, Paris, 1757. (Over 20 Or/Argent & well over 150 colour on colour).

FELS, Dr. Hans Richard von & SCHMID Dr. A., *Armorial de la ville de St-Gall*, Rorschach, 1952. (Over 30 Or/Argent and nearly 100 colour on colour).

FORAS, Comte Amédée de, *Armorial de Savoie*, Grenoble, 1883-1900. (Many Or/Argent).

FOSTER, Joseph, *Some Feudal Coats of Arms & Pedigrees*, London 1902, & in 1989 as *Dictionary of Heraldry*. (8 Or/Argent).

FOX-DAVIES, Arthur Charles, *A Complete Guide to Heraldry* London, Edinburgh, Paris, 1909 & 1969.

Franklyn, Julian, *Shield and Crest*, 1960. (9 Or/Argent, some blazoned "proper" which are clearly white).

GALBREATH, Donald Lindsay & JÉQUIER, Léon, *Lehrbuch der Heraldik*, Munich, 1978.

GELRE: B.R. *MS 15652-56*, Editions Ian van Helmont, Leuven, 1992.

GIBBON, John, *Introductio ad Latinam Blasoniam*, 1682 & 1962 (reprint by Cecil R. Humphery-Smith).

GRÜNENBERG, Conrad, *Wappenbuch 1452-1483* edited by Dr. R. Graf Stillfried-Alcantara & A. M. Hildebrandt, Görlitz, 1875.

GUÉRIN DE LA GRASSERIE, A. R., *Armorial de Bretagne*, Rennes,1845-48. (19 Or/Argent & over 50 colour on colour).

GUILLIM, John (1565-1621) *A Display of Heraldry*, London, 1611, sixth edition, 1724.

GUTMANN, Prof. Dr. S., *Ärzte und Apothekerwappen*, Spitzner Ettlingen, 1962-82.

HAIKONEN, Atte, *Finlands Kommunevapner*, Helsinki, 1970. (6 Or/Argent).

HANSEN SPERLING, John, *Arms on Monuments and Painted Glass in the Churches of Middlesex*, Cambridge, 1876.

HERALDRY INTERNATIONAL, *Heraldic Family Arms of Ireland*, Dublin, 1988.

HOF- & STAATSDRUCKEREI, K. & K., *Die Österreichisch-Ungarische Monarchie in Wort und Bild*, Wien, 1901.

HOWARD DE WALDEN, Lord, *Banners Standards and Badges from a Tudor Manuscript in the College of Arms*, London, 1904.

HUMPHERY-SMITH, Cecil R., owner of a manuscript 16th-century book of arms, time of Queen Elizabeth I.
"Heraldry in School Manuals of the Middle Ages" in *The Coat of Arms*, July & October 1960, Vol. VI, pp.115-123 & 163-170.
General Armory Two, London, 1973. (Over 30 Or/Argent)
Anglo-Norman Armory, Canterbury, 1975.
Anglo-Norman Armory Two, An Ordinary of Thirteenth Century Armorials, Canterbury, 1984. (14 Or/Argent).

HUPP, Otto, *Münchener Kalender*, 1885-1932.

JÄGER-SUNSTENAU, H., *General-Index zu den Siebmacher'schen Wappenbüchern 1605-1967*, Graz, 1964 & 1984.

JONES, Evan, *Medieval Heraldry*, Cardiff, 1943.

JOUGLAS DE MORENAS, Henri, *Grand Armorial de France*, 1934-40. (About 70 Or/Argent).

Kennedy's, Book of Arms, from the Records in Ulster's office 1816, Cecil R. Humphery-Smith, Canterbury, 1967.

KLINGSPOR, Carl Arvid von, *Baltisches Wappenbuch*, Stockholm, 1882. (More than 50 Or/Argent from 800).

KÖRNER, Dr. jur. Bernhard, *Handbuch der Heroldskunst*, 4 volumes, Görlitz, 1920-1930. (235 Or/Argent).

LAMPUGNANI, *Codice Trivulziano secolo XV*, since 1935 owned by the City of Milan in the Castello Sforzesco (Codex 1390). (More than 200 Or/Argent).

LARCHEZ, Lorédan, *Facsimile de l'Ancien Armorial équestre de la Toison d'Or et de l'Europe du XVe siècle* Paris, 1890.

LOUDA, Jiří, *European Civic Coats of Arms*, London, 1966. (Many Or/Argent).

LOUDA, Jiří & MACLAGAN, Michael, *Lines of Succession*, London, 1984.

LIŠKA, Karel, *Mestske Znaky s ozdobami*, Prague, 1989. (24 Or/Argent civic arms).

LOUTSCH, Dr. Jean-Claude, *Armorial du Pays de Luxembourg*, Luxembourg, 1974. (28 Or/Argent).

"Armorial Miltenberg fin XVe siècle", in *Archives Héraldiques Suisses*, 1989-92.

LYNDSAY OF THE MOUNT, Sir David, Lyon King of Arms, *Facsimile of an Ancient Heraldic Manuscript* (1542), 1878.

MAGNY, Marquis de, *La Science du Blason*, Paris, 1868. (11 Or/Argent).

MALTA, Sovrano Militare Ordine Gerosolimitano di, *Elenco storico della Nobiltà Italiana*, no date (circa 1960). (More than 300 Or/Argent).

MANDICH, Donald R. & PLACEK, Joseph A., *Russian Heraldry and Nobility*, Boynton Beach, Florida, 1992.

MARTINS ZÚQUETE, Doutor Alfonso Eduardo, *Armorial Lusitano*, Lisbon, 1961.

MASPOLI, Carlo, *Codice Carpani Stemmario quattrocentesco della Città e antica diocesi di Como*, Lugano, 1973. (45 Or/ Argent).

MÉNESTRIER, François-Claude, S.J., *Le véritable art du blason*, Lyons, 1659.
L'art du blason justifié, Lyons, 1661.
La science de la noblesse, Paris, 1691.
Neue Anleitung zu der sogenannten Herold-oder Wappenkunst, Ulm, 1694.

MERZ, Walter & HEGI, Friedrich, *Die Wappenrolle von Zürich*, facsimile edition, Zürich & Leipzig, 1930.

MEYER, Ed. Lorenz & TESDORPF, Oskar, *Hamburgische Wappen und Genealogien 1271*, 1888. (34 Or/Argent of 352, about 9%; 7 Vert/Or, about 2%).

MORGAN, Sylvanus, *Armilogia sive Ars chromatica*, London, 1666.

MULLINS, Thomas, *Irish Heraldic Scroll*, Dublin, 1962.

NEUFFORGE, Jacques de, *Armorial du Royaume des Pays-Bas*, Brussels.

OFFICER OF ARMS, *The Episcopal Arms of England & Wales*, London, 1906.

OSTROWSKI, Juliusz, *Ksiega Herbowna, Rodów Polskich*, Warsaw, 1904.

OSWALD, Gert, *Lexikon der Heraldik*, Mannheim, 1984. (over 20 Or/Argent).

PALIZZOLO GRAVINA, V., Barone di Ramione, *Il Blasone in Sicilia*, Palermo, 1871. (26 Or/Argent).

PAPWORTH, John W., *An Alphabetical Dictionary of Coats of Arms Belonging to Families in Great Britain and Ireland*, London,1874, known as, and republished as *Papworth's Ordinary of British Armorials*, Tabard, London,1961, (Over 200 Or/Argent).

PARDO DE GUEVARA y Valdés, Eduardo, *Manual de Heráldica Española*, Madrid, 1987.

PASTOUREAU, Michel, *Traité d'Héraldique*, Paris, 1979 & 1993.
Armorial des chevaliers de la Table Ronde, Paris, 1983.
Figures et Couleurs, Images et Symboles. Études sur la Symbolique et la Sensibilité Médiévales, Paris, 1986.

PETERSON, William, *Scottish Arms 1370-1678*, Edinburgh, 1881.

PETRA SANCTA, Silvester, S. J., *De symbolis heroicis*, Rome, 1634.
Tessarae Gentilitiae, Rome, 1638.

PIFERRER, Don Francisco, *Nobiliario de los Reinos y Señorios de España*, Madrid, 1857. (More than 140 Or/Argent).

POLSKIEJ AKADEMII NAUK, *Herby rycerstwa polskiego*, Kórnik, 1988.

RANEKE, Jan, *Svensk Adels-heraldik*, Malmö 1990. (2.5%, 7%).

RICHENTHAL, Ulrich von, *Das Concilium zu Constantz 1414-18*, facsimile edition, Merseburg, 1936. (40 Or/Argent).

RIDDARHUSDIREKTIONEN, *Sveriges Ridderskaps och Adels Kalender*, Stockholm, 1973. (Over 20 Or/Argent).

RIETSTAP, J. B., *Wapenboek van den Nederlandschen Adel*, Groningen, 1883. (See also Rolland: Illustrations).

RIQUER, Martí de, *Heraldica Catalana des l'any 1150 al 1550* Vols. I & II, Barcelona, 1883.

ROLLAND, Victor and Henri, *Illustrations to the Armorial General of Rietstap*, Heraldry Today, London, 1967. (In the six volumes more than 1500 Or/Argent).

ROSIER, Bernard du (Bernardus de Rosergio), *Liber Armorum*, Bibl. Nat. (Paris) lat. MS 6020 fol. 13-44.

ROTHE, Johannes, *Der Ritterspiegel*, 1386, edited by Hans Neumann, Halle/Saale, 1936.

ST JOHN HOPE, W., *The Stall Plates of Knights of the Garter* 1348-1485, 1902.

SALAMANCA, Armorial de, MS 2490. University Library of Salamanca.

SALAZAR y Castro, Instituto, *Blasonario de la Consanguinidad Ibérica*, Madrid, 1981. (30 Or/Argent).

SALENSON, Gheraert (ed.), *Le Jardin d'Armoiries*, Ghent, 1567.

SANTOS FERREIRA, G. L dos, *Armorial Portuguez*, Lisbon, 1920.

SAXOFERRATO, Bartolus de, *Tractatus de Insigniis*, 1350.

SCHÖLER, Eugen, *Historische Familienwappen in Franken* (Siebmacher's *Grosses Wappenbuch*, Band 7), Neustadt a.d. Aisch, 1975. (More than 70 Or/Argent only 30 Argent/Vert).

SCOTT-GILES, C. W., "Some Arthurian Coats of Arms", *The Coat of Arms, Vol. VIII*, 1965 & *Vol IX*, 1966.

SEYLER, Gustav A., *Geschichte der Heraldik*, Nuremberg, 1885-90.

SICILE, Herald of Alphonso V, King of Aragon, *Le Blason des Couleurs 1435-58*, published by Hippolite Cocheris, Paris, 1860.

SIDDONS, Michael Powell, *The Development of Welsh Heraldry*, Aberystwyth, 1991-1993.

SIEBMACHER, Johann, *Wappenbuch*, facsimile reprint of the 12 supplements from 1753-1806, Munich, 1979. (About 5% Or/Argent).

SILVEIRO PINTO, Albano da, *Rasenha das Familias Titulares e Grandes de Portugal*, Lisbon, 1883.

SMITH, Whitney (translated by Neubecker), *Zeichen der Menschen und Völker*, Lucerne, 1975.

SPENER, Philip Jacob, *Insignium Theoria*, Frankfurt, 1690.

SPERANSOV, N. N., *Coats of Arms of Russian Principalities* Moscow, 1974, (18 Or/Argent).

SPRETI, Marchese Vittorio, *Enciclopedia storico nobiliare*, Milan, 1928-35. (84% Or/Argent).

STADLER, Clemens, *Die Wappen der Niederbayrischen Landkreise*, Landshut. 1960. (15 Or/Argent).

STODART, R. R., *Scottish Arms, A collection of Armorial bearings A.D. 1370-1678 reproduced in facsimile from contemporary manuscripts*, Edinburgh, 1881.

STORCK, Herman, *Nyt Dansk Vaabenboq Adelslexikon*, Copenhagen, 1910.

STRÖHL, H. G., *Heraldischer Atlas*, Stuttgart, 1899.

SUOMEN Kunnallisliitto, *Municipal coats of arms ln Finland* Helsinki, 1970.

TOISON D'OR, Ancien armorial équestre et de l'Europe a XVe siècle facsimile, Paris, 1890.

TRETIAKOFF, Igor de, *Armorial de a Noblesse Russer,* Brussels, 1946.

VIDAL, Mgr. J. M. *Histoire des évêques de Pamiers*, Pamiers, 1926.

VIIKKOSANOMAT, *Tietoja Suomen Kapunqeista,* Information about Finnish boroughs, Keväällä, 1966.

VINCENT, Barthelemy, *Le Blason des Armoiries,* Lyon, 1581.

WILCZEK, Ferdinand Graf, *Wappen und Ahnentafeln,* 1983. (Over 40 Or/Argent).

WILSON, David M., *The Bayeux Tapestry,* New York, 1985.

WOODWARD, John, Rector of St Mary's Church, Montrose, & BURNETT, George, Lyon King of Arms, *A Treatise on Heraldry, British and Foreign*, London, 1892 (quoted from 1969 reprint).

ZELENKA, Ales, *Sudetendeutsches Wappenlexikon*, Passau, 1985. (Over 50 Or/Argent).

INDEX

Page references of arms illustrated in this work are in bold type.